DORLING KINDERSLEY 🕮 EYEWITNESS BOOKS

BIRD

Pheasant wing

Crow egg

Murre egg

Magpie egg

Peacock tail
covert

Wagtail nest

Mallard wing

Budgerigar feathers

EYEWITNESS BOOKS

Dunnock
egg

Great tit
egg

BIRD

Written by
DAVID BURNIE

Tawny
owl
skull

Mandarin duck
display feather

Quail egg

Swallow egg

European blackbird
skull

Golden
pheasant
cape feathers

Kittiwake egg

Macaw
flight feather

Avocet skull

Jay wing
feather

Bird of
paradise
display
feathers

Dorling Kindersley

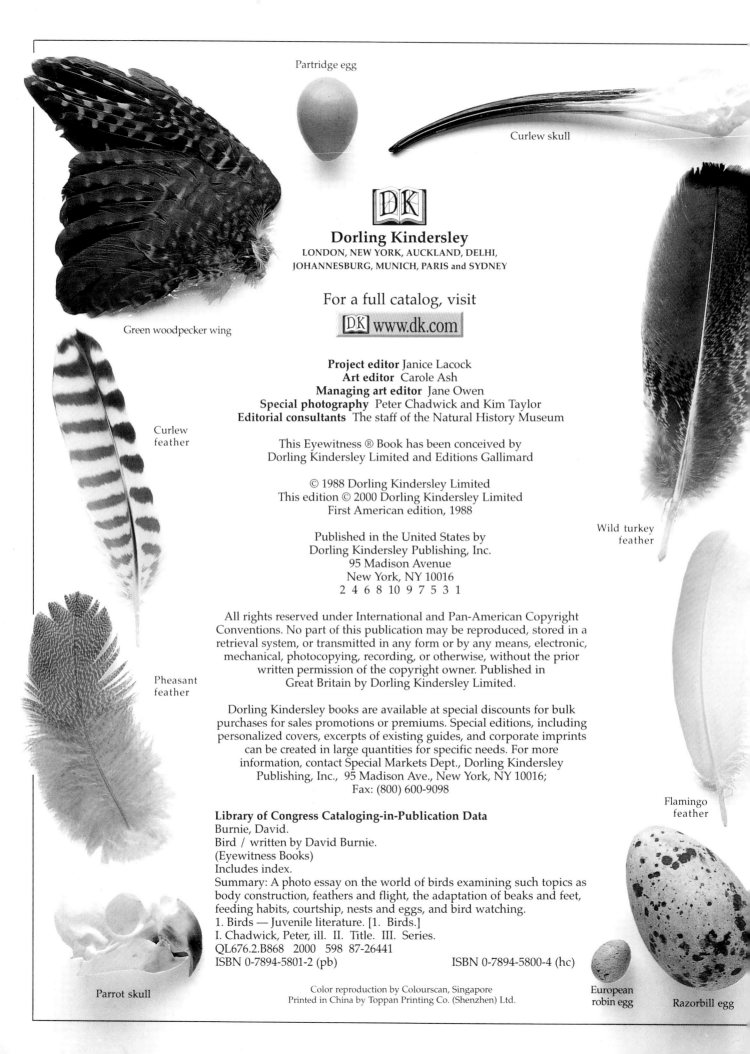

Partridge egg

Curlew skull

Green woodpecker wing

Curlew
feather

DK

Dorling Kindersley
LONDON, NEW YORK, AUCKLAND, DELHI,
JOHANNESBURG, MUNICH, PARIS and SYDNEY

For a full catalog, visit
DK www.dk.com

Project editor Janice Lacock
Art editor Carole Ash
Managing art editor Jane Owen
Special photography Peter Chadwick and Kim Taylor
Editorial consultants The staff of the Natural History Museum

This Eyewitness ® Book has been conceived by
Dorling Kindersley Limited and Editions Gallimard

© 1988 Dorling Kindersley Limited
This edition © 2000 Dorling Kindersley Limited
First American edition, 1988

Published in the United States by
Dorling Kindersley Publishing, Inc.
95 Madison Avenue
New York, NY 10016
2 4 6 8 10 9 7 5 3 1

Dorling Kindersley books are available at special discounts for bulk
purchases for sales promotions or premiums. Special editions, including
personalized covers, excerpts of existing guides, and corporate imprints
can be created in large quantities for specific needs. For more
information, contact Special Markets Dept., Dorling Kindersley
Publishing, Inc., 95 Madison Ave., New York, NY 10016;
Fax: (800) 600-9098

Pheasant
feather

Wild turkey
feather

Library of Congress Cataloging-in-Publication Data
Burnie, David.
Bird / written by David Burnie.
(Eyewitness Books)
Includes index.
Summary: A photo essay on the world of birds examining such topics as
body construction, feathers and flight, the adaptation of beaks and feet,
feeding habits, courtship, nests and eggs, and bird watching.
1. Birds — Juvenile literature. [1. Birds.]
I. Chadwick, Peter, ill. II. Title. III. Series.
QL676.2.B868 2000 598 87-26441
ISBN 0-7894-5801-2 (pb)   ISBN 0-7894-5800-4 (hc)

Flamingo
feather

Parrot skull

Color reproduction by Colourscan, Singapore
Printed in China by Toppan Printing Co. (Shenzhen) Ltd.

European
robin egg

Razorbill egg

Contents

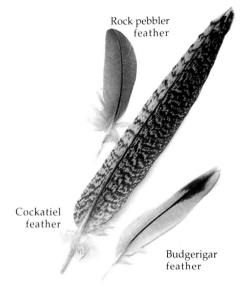

Rock pebbler feather

Cockatiel feather

Budgerigar feather

From dinosaur to bird

*Archaeopteryx -
the first bird*

Two HUNDRED MILLION YEARS AGO, at a time when insects were the only flying animals, a small lizard-like creature gave up scuttling between the trees in which it lived, and instead took to gliding. It did this on small flaps of skin that acted like parachutes, and from this humble beginning, giant winged reptiles called pterosaurs gradually evolved. But skin-like wings had their drawbacks: they were difficult to fold up when on the ground, and if they became torn, the chances of the creature being able to fly again were very small. Evolution's answer to this problem was the feather. In 1861, one of the world's most famous fossil animals, *Archaeopteryx*, was discovered. Although this creature lived over 150 million years ago, when the pterosaurs were still in their heyday, the fossils show that this crow-sized animal was thickly feathered. Unfortunately, nothing is known about the immediate descendants of *Archaeopteryx*. What is certain is that when the pterosaurs mysteriously died off with the dinosaurs, a huge increase in bird species followed. Today, over 8,500 species of birds populate the skies.

THE MISSING LINK

The five *Archaeopteryx* fossils found in Germany in 1861 all came from an area that was once flooded by a sea. When the animals died, their bodies were rapidly covered by silt which was so fine that it preserved not only the outlines of bones but also those of feathers. Over millions of years, this silt gradually packed down and became limestone, and when it was quarried, the stone yielded up its precious fossils. In this fossil, the birdlike wings and legs are clearly visible, as are the reptilian teeth and tail. Scientists think that *Archaeopteryx* evolved from small dinosaurs that ran upright instead of walking on all fours.

Wings

Tail

Legs

Teeth

Front view of a crow's skeleton

STAYING BALANCED

Compared to many animals, birds are compact creatures. A bird's legs, wings, and neck are all lightweight structures. The heavy parts, especially its wing and leg muscles, are packed closely around the rib cage and backbone. This allows a bird to stay balanced both on the wing and on the ground.

Skull

Neck

Backbone

Wishbone

Coracoid bone

Rib cage

Leg bones

EVOLUTIONARY EXPERIMENT

Although fossils show that pterosaurs were highly successful in their time, they all died out 65 million years ago. They were not directly related to the ancestors of modern birds.

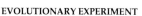

AS DEAD AS THE DODO

The dodo, shown here in the famous fictional encounter with Lewis Carroll's heroine, Alice, in *Through the Looking-Glass*, was one of many birds whose end was caused by humans. The dodo was a flightless bird of Madagascar and neighboring islands in the Indian Ocean. It was driven to extinction in the late 17th century. Flying birds have also suffered at human hands. The last passenger pigeon died in 1914. One hundred years earlier, the species had formed flocks over a billion strong.

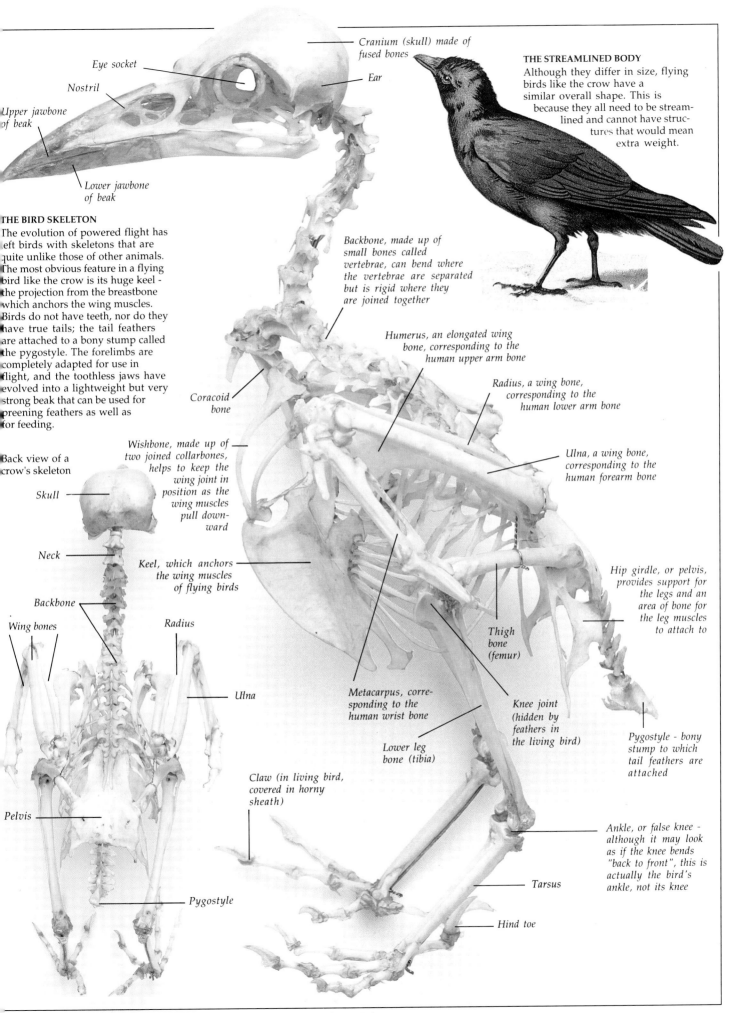

Eye socket

Nostril

Upper jawbone of beak

Cranium (skull) made of fused bones

Ear

Lower jawbone of beak

THE STREAMLINED BODY
Although they differ in size, flying birds like the crow have a similar overall shape. This is because they all need to be streamlined and cannot have structures that would mean extra weight.

THE BIRD SKELETON
The evolution of powered flight has left birds with skeletons that are quite unlike those of other animals. The most obvious feature in a flying bird like the crow is its huge keel - the projection from the breastbone which anchors the wing muscles. Birds do not have teeth, nor do they have true tails; the tail feathers are attached to a bony stump called the pygostyle. The forelimbs are completely adapted for use in flight, and the toothless jaws have evolved into a lightweight but very strong beak that can be used for preening feathers as well as for feeding.

Back view of a crow's skeleton

Skull

Neck

Backbone

Wing bones

Radius

Ulna

Pelvis

Pygostyle

Coracoid bone

Wishbone, made up of two joined collarbones, helps to keep the wing joint in position as the wing muscles pull downward

Keel, which anchors the wing muscles of flying birds

Backbone, made up of small bones called vertebrae, can bend where the vertebrae are separated but is rigid where they are joined together

Humerus, an elongated wing bone, corresponding to the human upper arm bone

Radius, a wing bone, corresponding to the human lower arm bone

Ulna, a wing bone, corresponding to the human forearm bone

Hip girdle, or pelvis, provides support for the legs and an area of bone for the leg muscles to attach to

Metacarpus, corresponding to the human wrist bone

Thigh bone (femur)

Knee joint (hidden by feathers in the living bird)

Pygostyle - bony stump to which tail feathers are attached

Lower leg bone (tibia)

Claw (in living bird, covered in horny sheath)

Ankle, or false knee - although it may look as if the knee bends "back to front", this is actually the bird's ankle, not its knee

Tarsus

Hind toe

Birds as animals

As A GROUP OF ANIMALS, birds have evolved a staggering range of body sizes. The smallest living bird, the bee humming-bird, weighs only 0.05 oz (1.6 g) and is dwarfed by many butterflies and moths in its rain forest home. The largest bird, the North African ostrich, has been known to weigh up to 275 lb (125 kg) - making it nearly 80,000 times heavier than its tiny and distant relative. Between these two extremes are the great majority of the Earth's birds - an enormous variety of species that have managed to colonize habitats as different as polar ice, and tropical rain forests.

Primary flight feathers

Alula

Secondary flight feathers

THE OUTER SURFACE
A bird's entire body, except its bill and feet, is usually covered with feathers. Some birds, such as vultures, have bare heads and necks.

Ear hidden beneath feathers

Nape

Mantle

Eye

Nostril

Upper jawbone of beak

Lower jawbone of beak

Breast

Secondary flight feathers

Alula (p. 10)

Primary flight feathers

Wing coverts

Rump

Flank

Upper-tail coverts (p. 18)

Toe

Under-tail coverts

Tail

Tarsus

Air sacs at base of neck

Trachea (windpipe)

BREATHING
Up to a fifth of a bird's body volume is taken up by air sacs that are connected to the lungs. The air sacs even extend into the wing bones.

Syrinx (a chamber which produces a bird's song)

Air sac extending into upper wing bone (humerus)

Air sacs within chest

Lungs

Air sacs in abdomen

THE DIGESTIVE SYSTEM
Because birds have no teeth, the digestive system has to break down all the food. In birds that eat plant matter, the gizzard grinds the food into a pulp.

Lung

Gullet

Kidney

Stomach

Crop

Gizzard

Heart

Liver

Pancreas

Oesophagus

Cloaca, the cavity where the intestinal and urinary ducts end

Small intestine

Gizzard chamber

THE GIZZARD
This muscular bag grinds up food, often with the help of stones that the bird swallows.

Ankle, or false knee

Tarsus

Hind toe

Claw

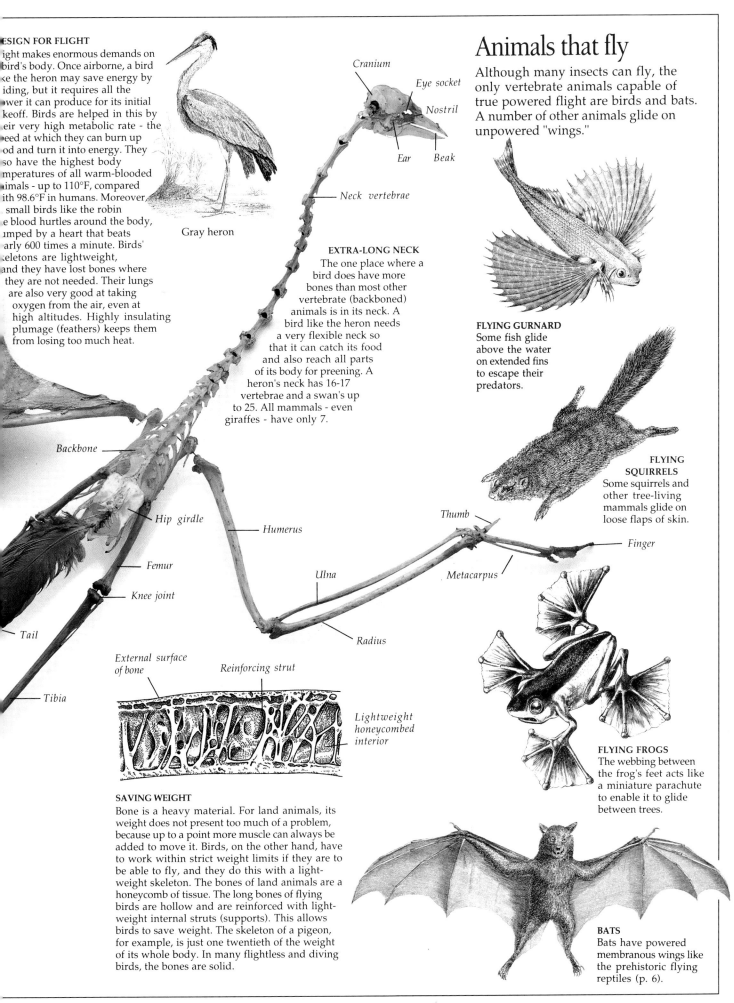

DESIGN FOR FLIGHT

Flight makes enormous demands on a bird's body. Once airborne, a bird like the heron may save energy by gliding, but it requires all the power it can produce for its initial takeoff. Birds are helped in this by their very high metabolic rate - the speed at which they can burn up food and turn it into energy. They also have the highest body temperatures of all warm-blooded animals - up to 110°F, compared with 98.6°F in humans. Moreover, in small birds like the robin the blood hurtles around the body, pumped by a heart that beats nearly 600 times a minute. Birds' skeletons are lightweight, and they have lost bones where they are not needed. Their lungs are also very good at taking oxygen from the air, even at high altitudes. Highly insulating plumage (feathers) keeps them from losing too much heat.

Gray heron

Cranium

Eye socket

Nostril

Ear   Beak

Neck vertebrae

EXTRA-LONG NECK

The one place where a bird does have more bones than most other vertebrate (backboned) animals is in its neck. A bird like the heron needs a very flexible neck so that it can catch its food and also reach all parts of its body for preening. A heron's neck has 16-17 vertebrae and a swan's up to 25. All mammals - even giraffes - have only 7.

Backbone

Hip girdle

Femur

Knee joint

Tail

Tibia

Humerus

Ulna

Radius

External surface of bone

Reinforcing strut

Lightweight honeycombed interior

SAVING WEIGHT

Bone is a heavy material. For land animals, its weight does not present too much of a problem, because up to a point more muscle can always be added to move it. Birds, on the other hand, have to work within strict weight limits if they are to be able to fly, and they do this with a light-weight skeleton. The bones of land animals are a honeycomb of tissue. The long bones of flying birds are hollow and are reinforced with light-weight internal struts (supports). This allows birds to save weight. The skeleton of a pigeon, for example, is just one twentieth of the weight of its whole body. In many flightless and diving birds, the bones are solid.

Animals that fly

Although many insects can fly, the only vertebrate animals capable of true powered flight are birds and bats. A number of other animals glide on unpowered "wings."

FLYING GURNARD
Some fish glide above the water on extended fins to escape their predators.

FLYING SQUIRRELS
Some squirrels and other tree-living mammals glide on loose flaps of skin.

Thumb

Finger

Metacarpus

FLYING FROGS
The webbing between the frog's feet acts like a miniature parachute to enable it to glide between trees.

BATS
Bats have powered membranous wings like the prehistoric flying reptiles (p. 6).

The wing

Oɴʟʏ ᴀ ꜰᴇᴡ ᴀɴɪᴍᴀʟꜱ - insects, bats, and birds - are capable of powered flight. Of these three, birds are by far the largest, fastest, and most powerful fliers. The secret of their success lies in the design of their wings. A bird's wing is light, strong, and flexible. It is also slightly curved from front to back, producing an airfoil profile, like an airplane wing, that pulls the bird upward as it flaps through the air. Although the size and shape of wings vary according to a bird's individual lifestyle, all share the same pattern, shown here in the wing of an owl.

OVER THE LIMIT
A bird's wings can bear its weight, plus light luggage such as food and nesting materials. Heavier loads, like human passengers, are strictly out of the question.

FLIGHT OF FANCY
Legend has it that as Icarus flew from Crete to Greece, he climbed too near the sun and the wax that held his feathers melted. But birds flying at high altitudes have to cope with quite different and much more real problems - thin air, little oxygen, and intense cold.

MECHANICAL MIMICRY
Leonardo da Vinci (1452-1519) drew on his knowledge of bird wings to design machines that would imitate their flight. He replaced bones with wood, tendons with ropes, and feathers with sailcloth. As far as is known, none of these devices ever got beyond his drawing board. Anyway, they would have been far too heavy to fly.

FLAPPING FAILURES
The heroic birdmen of bygone days did not realize that flapping flight would always be beyond the power of human muscles. True man-powered flight has been achieved only through the later invention of the propeller.

ALULA
This group of feathers is held open in slow flight to prevent stalling.

PRIMARY FLIGHT FEATHERS
The "primaries" produce the power for flight as the bird brings its wings downward. The outermost primaries can be used for steering, like the flaps on a plane's wing.

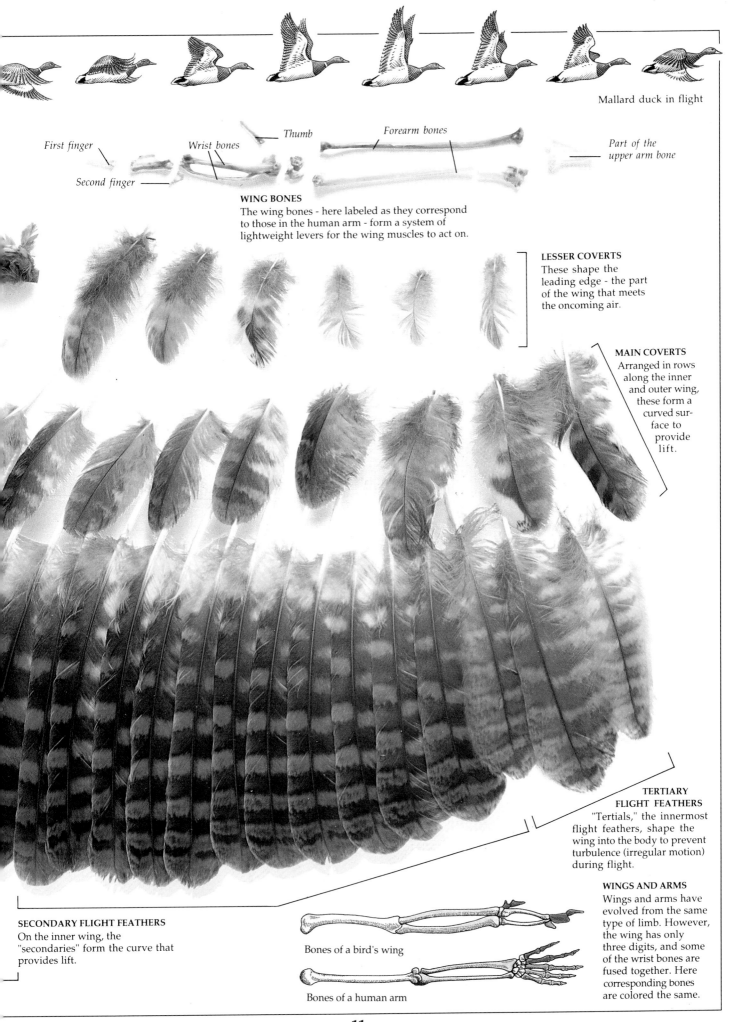

Mallard duck in flight

First finger

Second finger

Wrist bones

Thumb

Forearm bones

Part of the upper arm bone

WING BONES
The wing bones - here labeled as they correspond to those in the human arm - form a system of lightweight levers for the wing muscles to act on.

LESSER COVERTS
These shape the leading edge - the part of the wing that meets the oncoming air.

MAIN COVERTS
Arranged in rows along the inner and outer wing, these form a curved surface to provide lift.

TERTIARY FLIGHT FEATHERS
"Tertials," the innermost flight feathers, shape the wing into the body to prevent turbulence (irregular motion) during flight.

WINGS AND ARMS
Wings and arms have evolved from the same type of limb. However, the wing has only three digits, and some of the wrist bones are fused together. Here corresponding bones are colored the same.

SECONDARY FLIGHT FEATHERS
On the inner wing, the "secondaries" form the curve that provides lift.

Bones of a bird's wing

Bones of a human arm

Maneuverability and fast takeoff

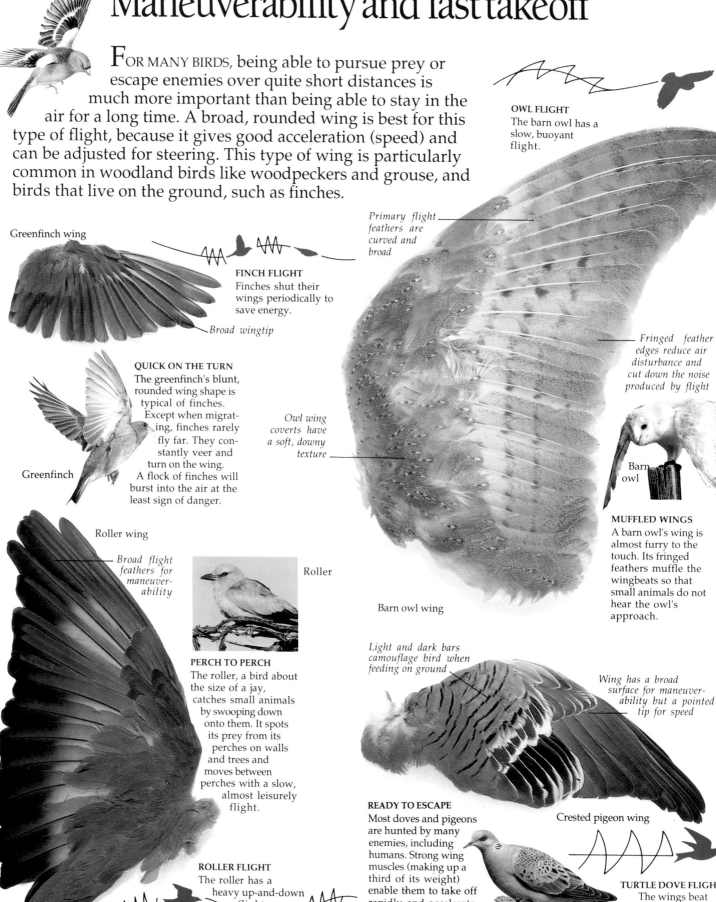

FOR MANY BIRDS, being able to pursue prey or escape enemies over quite short distances is much more important than being able to stay in the air for a long time. A broad, rounded wing is best for this type of flight, because it gives good acceleration (speed) and can be adjusted for steering. This type of wing is particularly common in woodland birds like woodpeckers and grouse, and birds that live on the ground, such as finches.

OWL FLIGHT
The barn owl has a slow, buoyant flight.

Greenfinch wing

FINCH FLIGHT
Finches shut their wings periodically to save energy.

Broad wingtip

QUICK ON THE TURN
The greenfinch's blunt, rounded wing shape is typical of finches. Except when migrating, finches rarely fly far. They constantly veer and turn on the wing. A flock of finches will burst into the air at the least sign of danger.

Greenfinch

Primary flight feathers are curved and broad

Owl wing coverts have a soft, downy texture

Fringed feather edges reduce air disturbance and cut down the noise produced by flight

Barn owl

MUFFLED WINGS
A barn owl's wing is almost furry to the touch. Its fringed feathers muffle the wingbeats so that small animals do not hear the owl's approach.

Barn owl wing

Roller wing

Broad flight feathers for maneuverability

Roller

PERCH TO PERCH
The roller, a bird about the size of a jay, catches small animals by swooping down onto them. It spots its prey from its perches on walls and trees and moves between perches with a slow, almost leisurely flight.

ROLLER FLIGHT
The roller has a heavy up-and-down flight.

Light and dark bars camouflage bird when feeding on ground

Wing has a broad surface for maneuverability but a pointed tip for speed

READY TO ESCAPE
Most doves and pigeons are hunted by many enemies, including humans. Strong wing muscles (making up a third of its weight) enable them to take off rapidly and accelerate to 50 mph (80 kph).

Crested pigeon wing

TURTLE DOVE FLIGH
The wings beat rapidly withou pauses.

Turtle dove

Woodpecker wing

Green coloring for camouflage

WOODPECKER FLIGHT
Woodpeckers climb and dive much more steeply than most other birds.

Pheasants in flight

Pheasant wing

Folded flight feathers

STEERING A SAFE COURSE
In dense forests, a green woodpecker needs short, rounded wings so that it can turn suddenly to avoid obstacles. Its wing shape also helps it come to a controlled landing when approaching a tree.

Woodpecker

Camouflaged inner wing feathers conceal bird on ground

VERTICAL TAKEOFF
Pheasants are reluctant fliers. If alarmed, they take off almost vertically on their broad wings. Once airborne, they then glide away in a straight line.

Camouflaged plumage found only on the female

FLYING FOR COVER
Grouse, like pheasants and other game birds, spend most of their time on the ground. On sensing danger, they first crouch down. Then - waiting almost till the last moment - they spring upward, at the same time bringing their opened wings sharply downward, to burst into the air. Grouse fly by alternating rapid wingbeats with short glides and only cover a short distance before landing. In nearly all game birds, the female's wings are camouflaged and the male's are more noticeable.

PHEASANT FLIGHT
Rapid wingbeats are followed by a long glide.

Female black grouse or "blackhen"

Female black grouse or "blackhen" wing

Long flight feathers allow the grouse to glide

Male black grouse or "blackcock" wing

Speed and endurance

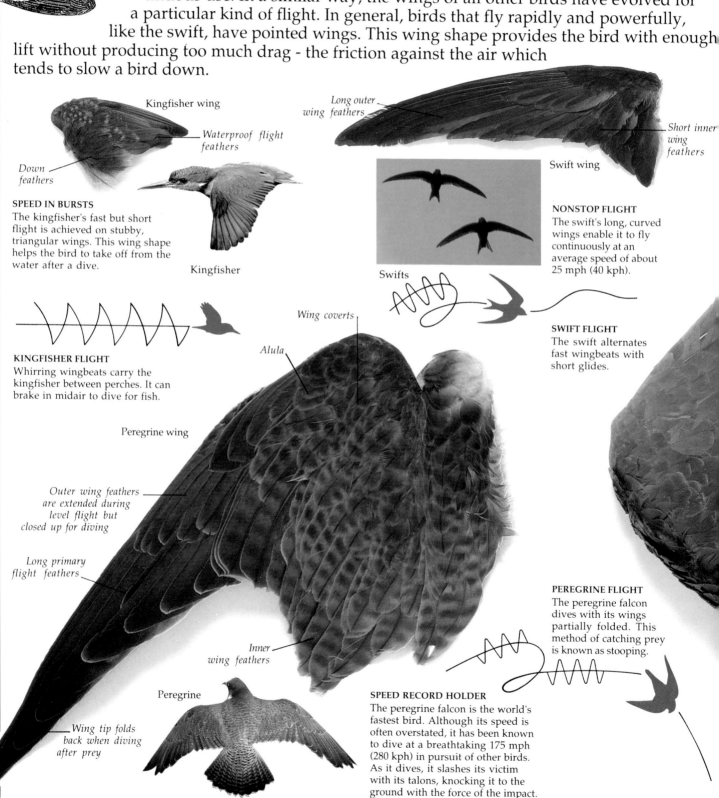

WHEN A SWIFT makes its first brief landing before nesting, it brings to an end a flight that may have lasted nonstop for three years. The swift is just one of a number of birds that land only to breed, and its slender, curved wings are completely adapted for continuous use. In a similar way, the wings of all other birds have evolved for a particular kind of flight. In general, birds that fly rapidly and powerfully, like the swift, have pointed wings. This wing shape provides the bird with enough lift without producing too much drag - the friction against the air which tends to slow a bird down.

Kingfisher wing

Waterproof flight feathers

Down feathers

SPEED IN BURSTS
The kingfisher's fast but short flight is achieved on stubby, triangular wings. This wing shape helps the bird to take off from the water after a dive.

Kingfisher

Long outer wing feathers

Short inner wing feathers

Swift wing

NONSTOP FLIGHT
The swift's long, curved wings enable it to fly continuously at an average speed of about 25 mph (40 kph).

Swifts

KINGFISHER FLIGHT
Whirring wingbeats carry the kingfisher between perches. It can brake in midair to dive for fish.

SWIFT FLIGHT
The swift alternates fast wingbeats with short glides.

Wing coverts

Alula

Peregrine wing

Outer wing feathers are extended during level flight but closed up for diving

Long primary flight feathers

Inner wing feathers

Peregrine

Wing tip folds back when diving after prey

PEREGRINE FLIGHT
The peregrine falcon dives with its wings partially folded. This method of catching prey is known as stooping.

SPEED RECORD HOLDER
The peregrine falcon is the world's fastest bird. Although its speed is often overstated, it has been known to dive at a breathtaking 175 mph (280 kph) in pursuit of other birds. As it dives, it slashes its victim with its talons, knocking it to the ground with the force of the impact.

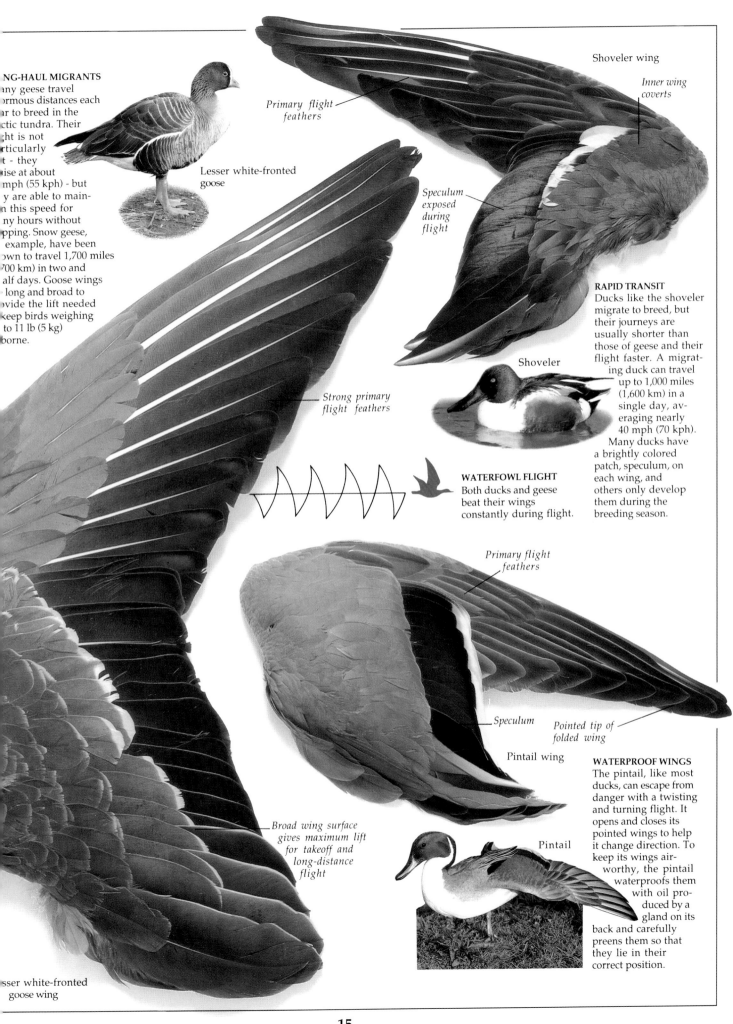

LONG-HAUL MIGRANTS
[Ma]ny geese travel [en]ormous distances each [yea]r to breed in the [arc]tic tundra. Their [fli]ght is not [par]ticularly [fas]t - they [cru]ise at about [...]mph (55 kph) - but [the]y are able to main[tai]n this speed for [ma]ny hours without [sto]pping. Snow geese, [for] example, have been [kn]own to travel 1,700 miles [(2,7]00 km) in two and [a h]alf days. Goose wings [are] long and broad to [pro]vide the lift needed [to]keep birds weighing [up]to 11 lb (5 kg) [air]borne.

Lesser white-fronted goose

Primary flight feathers

Shoveler wing

Inner wing coverts

Speculum exposed during flight

RAPID TRANSIT
Ducks like the shoveler migrate to breed, but their journeys are usually shorter than those of geese and their flight faster. A migrating duck can travel up to 1,000 miles (1,600 km) in a single day, averaging nearly 40 mph (70 kph). Many ducks have a brightly colored patch, speculum, on each wing, and others only develop them during the breeding season.

Shoveler

Strong primary flight feathers

WATERFOWL FLIGHT
Both ducks and geese beat their wings constantly during flight.

Primary flight feathers

Speculum

Pointed tip of folded wing

Pintail wing

Broad wing surface gives maximum lift for takeoff and long-distance flight

Pintail

WATERPROOF WINGS
The pintail, like most ducks, can escape from danger with a twisting and turning flight. It opens and closes its pointed wings to help it change direction. To keep its wings airworthy, the pintail waterproofs them with oil produced by a gland on its back and carefully preens them so that they lie in their correct position.

[Le]sser white-fronted goose wing

Soaring, gliding, and hovering

Hummingbirds, the smallest flying birds, hover while feeding

WHEN A BIRD FLAPS ITS WINGS, it uses up a great deal of energy - about 15 times as much as when it is sitting still. But some birds have managed to evolve ways of flying that take much less effort than this. Large birds do it by soaring and gliding - harnessing the power of the sun or the wind to keep them in the air. Right at the other extreme is hovering - keeping still in the air by beating the wings nonstop, just as a swimmer treads water to stay afloat.

Narrow wing provides lift without too much drag during gliding

Great black-backed gull wing

GLIDING GULLS
Slender, pointed wings enable gulls to glide on updrafts - currents of air forced upward by cliffs and hillsides. The lift generated by these updrafts is enough to support birds as heavy as the great black-backed gull, which weighs over 4.5 lb (2 kg).

Great black-backed gull

GULL FLIGHT
In flapping flight, a gull may travel at 25 mph (40 kph), but in a strong updraft, it can stay motionless over the ground.

Inner wing coverts mould wing to the body

"Slotted" primary flight feathers reduce disturbances

Kestrel wing

HANGING IN THE AIR
Although many birds can hover momentarily, few can keep up this type of flight, as it is very tiring. One exception is the kestrel, which hovers as its keen eyes pinpoint small animals from high overhead. It needs a slight head wind to help keep it up.

Kestrel

KESTREL FLIGHT
The kestrel has the fluttering forward flight typical of falcons.

KESTREL HOVERING
The wings beat rapidly and the tail is fanned out to provide lift as the wind blows past.

Birds that cannot fly

Millions of years ago, giant flightless birds roamed the Earth. Today only a few dozen smaller species survive.

Penguin flipper

Stiff wing blade acts as a propeller

Densely packed feathers

WINGS AS FLIPPERS
Penguins swim by "flying" underwater with their wings. One species, the emperor penguin, can dive up to 800 ft (250 m) using its wings to move forward. Penguins' wings cannot be folded up like those of most birds.

Adelie penguins in Antarctica

Rhea wing

Rhea

Inner wing

Downy feathers provide insulation but cannot produce lift

Outer wing

PAMPAS RUNNER
Rheas are the South American counterparts of ostriches. Their wing feathers are long, but useless for flight.

THE HEAVIEST BIRD
Ornithologists - scientists who study birds - calculate that no bird heavier than 40 lb (18 kg) can fly. Above that weight, muscle power would never be enough to keep a bird airborne. The African ostrich, weighing in at 260 lb (120 kg), is nearly seven times over this limit. Its wings are no more than weak flaps with a fan of 16 fluffy flight feathers. Although the ostrich cannot fly, it can run at speeds of over 30 mph (50 kph) and overtake many flying birds.

Straight leading edge is held slanting upward during soaring

Primary flight feathers are used for maneuvering

Splayed (extended) "fingers" help to reduce air disturbances

Broad inner flight feathers provide lift as bird soars within a thermal

Buzzard wing

Buzzard

UP WITHOUT EFFORT
Heavy birds of prey like the buzzard soar on thermals - columns of warm, rising air. They need flapping flight only to get from one thermal to the next.

BUZZARD FLIGHT
All soaring birds bank (turn) tightly to keep within the rising air of a thermal.

Tails

DURING the course of evolution, birds have gradually lost the part of the backbone that in other animals makes up the tail, and have replaced it with feathers. The size of these feathers differs from bird to bird. Some birds like murres and puffins hardly have any tail at all. Others like peacocks and male birds of paradise have tails that are so long they make flight quite difficult.

Tail fanned on approach; body held horizontally

Landing; feet held forward to grasp perch

Tail closed as bird settles on perch

AIR BRAKE
When a bird comes in to land, it lowers and spreads out its tail feathers. The feathers act as a brake and slow the bird's approach.

RUMP FEATHERS
Above the base of a wood pigeon's tail, the rump feathers provide insulation with their thick down.

Wood pigeon

TAIL COVERTS
Dense rows of these feathers lie over the base of the bird's tail and smooth the air-flow over it.

TAIL FEATHERS
The wood pigeon, like most birds, has 12 tail feathers. The feather tips get frayed by the wear and tear of flight.

Tips worn and frayed by flight

Tail shapes

Flight puts many restrictions on a bird's shape. For this reason, birds that spend much of their time flying almost always have lightweight, streamlined tails. But other birds, especially those that live on the ground or in forests, have evolved tails that are shaped for uses other than flight. Some of these are used for balance, some for perching, and others for attracting the attention of a mate.

Magpie

A TAIL FOR BALANCE

The central feathers in a magpie's tail are nearly 10 in (25 cm) long. Long tails are normally used for display (pp. 28-29), but because both male and female magpies have them, it is more likely that they are used for balancing on the ground or clambering in trees.

Rump feathers

Tail coverts

Elongated tail feathers

Magpie tail

Green woodpecker tail

Rump feathers

Great spotted woodpecker

Tail coverts

Stiff quills

Great spotted woodpecker

Rump feathers

Tail coverts

Sharp points created by rubbing of tail against trees

Rump feathers showing distinctive orange coloration, revealed during flight

Crossbill tail

Tail coverts

Fork to aid maneuverability

FORKED TAILS

In some birds, the central tail feathers are the longest. In others, particularly many of the finches, the situation is reversed and the tail has a forked shape. This arrangement probably gives small birds greater ability to maneuver.

Crossbill

Downy black-tipped rump feathers lying above tail coverts

Tail coverts

Curved tail feathers used in display by male

Black grouse tail

TAILS FOR SUPPORT

A woodpecker uses its tail to brace itself as it climbs the trunk of a tree. Woodpecker tail feathers are unusually stiff so that they can support a large amount of the bird's weight. Being subjected to rather rough treatment, the tips of the feathers rapidly wear down.

Male pheasant with wing and tail feathers revealed during takeoff

A TAIL FOR DISPLAY

In the black grouse, the male's tail feathers are crescent shaped, and the female's are straight. Differences like this are a sure sign that the tail has evolved this shape for display rather than for flight.

Black grouse

Peacock

The structure of feathers

FEATHERS are the great evolutionary development that separates birds from all other animals. A humming-bird's plumage may number under 1,000 feathers; and a large bird like the swan may have over 25,000, with nearly four fifths of these covering the head and neck alone. Like hair, claws, and horns, feathers are made from a protein called keratin. It is this substance that gives them their great strength and flexibility. But for all their complex structure, fully grown feathers are quite dead. As feathers develop, they split apart to form a mesh of filaments that link together. Once this has happened, their blood supply is cut off. The feathers then serve their time, unless lost by accident, and when worn out they are finally discarded during molting.

BREAKABLE PLUMAGE
A Central American motmot changes the shape of its tail feathers during preening. When it pecks at a tail feather, the feather's barbs break off to leave a bare shaft ending in a spoon-shaped tip. Why it does this has not yet been discovered.

Feather sheaths

Emerging feather tufts

Growing feathers within sheaths

Fully grown feathers after the protective sheaths have fallen away

HOW FEATHERS GROW
Feathers start their growth as pulp inside tubes known as feather sheaths. The tip of a feather gradually emerges from the growing sheath, unrolling and splitting apart to form a flat blade. Eventually the feather sheath falls away, leaving the fully formed feather.

Quill tip embedded in skin and attached to muscles

FEATHER SHAFT
The hollow shaft contains the dried remains of the pulp.

Hollow interior

Pulp from interior of shaft

PEOPLE AND FEATHERS
Feathers have long been used by people for decoration and for more practical purposes. Headdresses and quill pens made use of flight feathers. The down feathers of ducks and geese are still used for bedding, and the brilliantly colored plumes of some tropical birds find their way into objects such as fishing flies.

Quill

FILOPLUMES
These hairlike growths, found between the feathers on a bird's body, help a bird to detect how its feathers are lying.

Barbs

Quill

SPLIT FEATHERS
Some feathers are split to form two different halves attached to the same shaft. This enables a single feather to perform two different functions.

Aftershaft, second shaft from a single quill

A SURFACE FOR FLIGHT
To work effectively, a flight feather has to form a single continuous surface for air to flow over. This surface is produced by thousands of barbules. These lie on either side of each barb and lock together as hooks and catches. If barbule hooks come loose, a bird simply preens them back into position with its beak.

Barbule

Hook

Catch

Barb

Feather tip

Notch for reducing air disturbance (p. 24)

Outer vane (faces into the wind)

Rachis, or shaft

Downcurved edge

Upcurved edge

Inner vane (faces away from the wind)

Parallel barbs locked together to form a smooth surface

Further magnification of macaw feather

FEATHERS WITHIN FEATHERS
Under high magnification, barbs and barbules look almost like miniature feathers. On flight feathers like this, the barbs are closely packed and the barbules are short and numerous. By contrast, on down feathers there are fewer barbs but they are much longer. It is not unusual for them to have no barbules at all (p. 26).

Scarlet macaw flight feather magnified to show barbs and barbules

Feather care

Feathers receive a tremendous battering during daily use. They also become dirty and infested with parasites such as feather lice. Most feathers are shed every year during molting, but birds still spend a lot of time making sure their plumage stays in a good condition. They do this by preening - using the beak like a comb to draw together the barbs and barbules - and also by special methods of feather care, such as oiling, powdering, and bathing, both in water and in dust.

POWDERED PLUMAGE
Egrets, herons, and some other birds have special feathers that break up to form a powder. This "powder down" is used to keep the plumage in good condition. Unlike other feathers, powder down feathers never stop growing.

ANTING JAYS
Jays sometimes encourage ants to swarm over their feathers. Poisonous formic acid produced by the ants may drive out parasites in the jay's plumage.

DUST BATHS
Dust both absorbs and scrapes things away. Bathing in dust scours dirt from a bird's feathers.

Feathers

THE FEATHERS that make up a bird's plumage are of four main types: down feathers, body feathers, tail feathers, and wing feathers. Although many of them are drab and dull, others are beautifully shaped and colored structures.

DOWN FEATHERS
Soft, finely divided feathers trap a layer of air to provide insulation.

Peacock

Pigeon

BODY FEATHERS
The feathers that stream-line a bird's body.

Macaw

African gray parrot

Red lory

Parrots

Macaws

TAIL FEATHERS
Feathers for steering, balance, and display.

Goose

Goose

Flamingo

Peacock

Pheasants

Peacock

Palawan

Golden pheasant

INNER WING FEATHERS
Feathers that smooth the flow of air over the bird's wing.

Hummingbird

Guinea fowl

Reeve's pheasant

Flamingo

Grouse

Lady Amherst's pheasant

Grouse

Pheasant

Goose

Wild turkey

Pheasant

Macaw

Macaw

Guinea fowl

OUTER WING FEATHERS
The strongest feathers in a bird's plumage, shaped to provide the power for flight.

Forktail

Gull

Macaw

Crimson rosella

Lesser spotted woodpecker

Crimson rosella

Orioles

Gull

Turkey

Aricara

Parakeet

Black-bird

Wing feathers

THE WING FEATHERS are one of the most important parts of a bird's flying machinery. They combine strength with lightness and flexibility. Compared with the rest of the body, the wings have relatively few feathers, but each one is important, working with its neighbors to form a perfect surface for flight.

The outer wing

The long feathers of the outer wing provide most of the bird's flight power and keep it from stalling. The outermost flight feathers help a bird to steer by spreading open or closing up in flight.

Barn owl

Green woodpecker

Jay

Adult starling

Young starling

OUTER COVERTS
By overlapping the bases of the flight feathers, the coverts smooth the flow of air.

LOPSIDED DESIGN
Nearly all flight feathers are like this cockateel's - narrower on their leading edge. This design produces lift as the feather slices through the air.

GRADED SHAPES
Away from the wing-tip, the flight feathers become gradually shorter and broader. These are from a regent parrot.

Wider trailing edge

Slot

Narrow leading edge

HEAVY-DUTY FEATHERS
The mute swan, which weighs up to 26 lb (12 kg), needs especially long and strong feathers to power its flight. Its outer wing feathers can be up to 18 in (45 cm) long but even so, each feather weighs only 0.5 oz (14 g).

Fringe

Tawny owl

Barn owl

Swan

ABOVE AND BELOW
Many wing feathers are different colors underneath. Macaws' feathers bend light to produce shimmery colors - in this species, blue above and yellow below.

SILENT FEATHERS
Fringes on the edges of owl feathers break up the flow of air and silence the owl's flight, as shown on this tawny owl feather.

SLOTTED FEATHERS
The deep slot in this crow feather forms a gap in the wing that reduces irregular motion.

The inner wing

Inner wing feathers are generally shorter than those on the outer wing. They are not subject to so much force during flight and, for this reason, their quills are shorter and the feathers are less well anchored. With the exception of some display feathers, they are also more evenly shaped than outer wing feathers.

A BALANCED BLADE

Inner wing feathers, here the regent parrot's, point away from the wind, not across it. They therefore do not need a lopsided shape to provide lift like the outer wing feathers.

IN-FLIGHT MARKINGS

The bright colors of many birds, such as budgerigars, are revealed only when the wings are fully open.

THE MANDARIN DUCK'S SAIL

The male mandarin duck has a pair of these extraordinary sail feathers - one at the base of each wing. They are shown off during courtship.

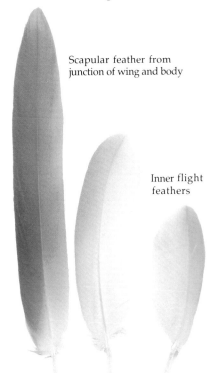

Scapular feather from junction of wing and body

Inner flight feathers

COLORED BY ITS FOOD

The greater flamingo lives on a diet of shrimps and other crustaceans. From these it extracts a pink dye that is taken into its feathers.

Curlew   Mallard   Jay

AT THE BOUNDARY

Flight feathers at the boundary between the inner and outer wing have curved quills and blunt tips. They may have bright patterns that show up in flight.

CAMOUFLAGED FEATHERS

Patterned brown feathers hide the woodcock from enemies (p. 30).

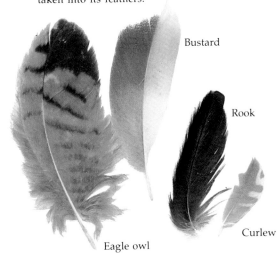

Bustard

Rook

Curlew

Eagle owl

UNDERWING FEATHERS

Like the upperwing coverts, these lie close together to smooth the flow of air. Their surface is concave (curved in), rather than convex (curved out) as in the upper wing.

INFREQUENT FLIERS

This feather is from a wild turkey. Like many birds that live on the ground, it rarely uses its feathers for flight.

INNER COVERTS

The inner coverts, in this case from a buzzard, overlap the front feathers of the inner wing. Their down shows that they are also used for insulating the body when the wing is folded.

Body, down, and tail feathers

FEATHERS are not only designed for flight. They also insulate and waterproof a bird's body and enable it to conceal itself, attract a mate, incubate its eggs, and stay balanced when on the ground. All these tasks are performed by three types of feathers: body feathers, down feathers, and the feathers in the tail. The way these feathers work depends on their shape and whether or not their barbs can lock together.

Down feathers

Down feathers are found next to the bird's skin. Their barbs do not lock together but instead spread out to form a soft, irregular mass. Down is one of the most effective insulating materials found in the animal kingdom.

— Barb

— Quill

UNLOCKED BARBS
In this peacock down feather, the separate barbs can be seen. These barbs trap air, which forms an insulation layer below the body feathers.

Body feathers

Body feathers come in a huge range of shapes and sizes. Some are used just to insulate and cover the bird's body, but others have developed for display (pp. 28-29) and have evolved bright colors or strange shapes.

THERMAL CLADDING
Small down feathers like this one from a partridge are packed together tightly on the bird's body to form a furlike mat.

FEATHERS FOR INCUBATION
Many birds, including the teal, pull out breast feathers to insulate their eggs. Some are collected and sold for bedding.

DUAL-FUNCTION FEATHER
Many feathers have a mass of down near the point where they are attached to the body, as shown on this silver pheasant feather.

Red lory feathers

African gray parrot feathers

Macaw feathers

PATTERNS ON THE SURFACE
In many boldly patterned birds, only the exposed tips of the feathers show distinctive markings - the rest of the feather is dull, as on this pheasant.

TROPICAL BRILLIANCE
Brilliant and varied body colors are more common in birds that live in the tropics than those that live in moderate regions. Bright colors may help birds to identify their own kind among the many others that share their habitat.

COURTSHIP PLUMES
Some birds have evolved body feathers that are completely adapted for a role in attracting a mate. These hanging feathers adorn the neck of the male wild turkey. Each feather is divided into a pair of plumes.

Long quill —

Shortened barbs

FLYING HEAVYWEIGHT
This body feather comes from a bustard, one of the world's heaviest flying birds.

LEAFY CAMOUFLAGE
The dull green tips of the green woodpecker's body feathers are ideal camouflage against the woodland leaves of its natural habitat.

A PHEASANT'S CAPE
The neck feathers of the male golden pheasant form a brilliant black-and-gold cape. These feathers were once highly prized by fishermen for use in fishing flies.

Tail feathers

Birds use their tails for three things - to steer them during flight, to balance when perched on the ground, and to impress a mate or a rival during courtship. Because of this, tail feathers come in a great range of shapes, sizes and colors, something that is especially noticeable in breeding male birds.

A CURLED TAIL
The male mallard has two distinctive curled feathers at the base of his tail. When he courts a mate, he throws his head up and shows off his plumage. The female's tail feathers are straight.

EYED FEATHERS
The "eyes" on the peacock's tail extend right down to the short feathers at the tail's base, making a spectacular courtship display.

Growing feather

Mature feather

Feather sheath

— Quill

YOUNG AND OLD
Here, a growing tail feather from a kestrel is shown alongside a fully grown one. Both feathers are from a bird molting into adult plumage.

STRESS BARS
The light-colored bars in this parrot's tail feather are caused by changes in diet that occurred during the feather's growth.

BRED FOR COLOR
Varied colors in budgerigars are the result of controlled breeding. Wild budgerigars are blue and green; other colors are found only in birds bred under control.

THE TAIL'S SIDES
The feathers that are farthest from the center of the tail are the least evenly shaped because, when the tail is fanned in the air, the outer feathers must provide lift when air flows across them. These lopsided tail feathers are from a curlew.

CENTRAL TAIL FEATHER
This even owl feather comes from the center of the tail.

IRIDESCENT TAILS
Magpies have long tail feathers that look black from a distance but seem colored when seen from nearby. As in the macaw's flight feathers (p. 24), this effect is caused by the bending of light.

GAME BIRD TAILS
The tails of male pheasants, chickens, and other game birds can be exceptionally long. Even this long feather from a pheasant's tail would be dwarfed by that of a Japanese red jungle fowl: its tail feathers have been bred to reach 35 ft (10.7 m).

Pheasant

Count Raggi's
bird of
paradise

Courtship

THE WAYS IN WHICH BIRDS FIND PARTNERS and mate is one of the most fascinating and colorful features of all animal life. Although divorce may be rare in birds, almost every other imaginable marriage arrangement exists somewhere in the bird world. Having fought off other males, often by establishing a territory, some males attract a single mate and remain faithful to her for life. At the other extreme, some males use their brilliant courtship plumage to attract a whole series of mates, deserting each one in favor of the next as soon as mating has taken place. Birds attract their mates by a combination of visible signals that range from special plumage to brightly colored legs and inflatable pouches. They also use ritual movements that can be as simple as a gull's nod of the head or as bizarre as the display of the male great bustard, who throws back his wings and head and looks like he's turning his head inside out.

ROLE REVERSAL
Oddly for a bird, the female red phalarope courts the male. She is the more brightly colored of the two birds.

THE PEACOCK'S TAIL
Peacocks are members of the pheasant family, a group of birds that show some of the most spectacular and elaborate courtship plumage in the bird world.

HIDDEN SUPPORT
From the back, the upright feathers of the peacock's "true" tail can be seen. These brace the much longer and more brilliant tail coverts.

ON PARADE
Male lyrebirds make themselves arenas on which they strut and display. Their movements attract a series of mates.

Feathers without ———
barbules (p. 21) do not interlock, so appear lacy

——— *Tip of quill*

MYSTERY SOLVED

t was only in the last century that naturalists xplored the forests of New Guinea and saw ow plumes like this from a Count Raggi's bird of aradise were used by male irds. In displays, during which they hang pside down, the irds throw heir plumes pen.

Body feathers

Streaked central feather

INFLATABLE ATTRACTION
The male frigate bird has a stunning red throat pouch that he uses to attract a mate. He keeps his pouch inflated for many hours until a female, lured by this irresistible courtship device, joins him.

DEFUSING TENSION
Although boobies and gannets nest in densely packed colonies, each bird will stab at any neighbor who dares to intrude on its small but very private "patch." When pairs meet, courtship ceremonies are needed to reduce these aggressive instincts. Here two blue-footed boobies join in the "pelican" display, pointing their beaks out of each other's way.

IN STEP WITH THE SEASON
The brilliant colors on puffins' beaks are at their brightest during the breeding season in early summer. The color lies in a horny sheath that covers the out-side of the beak. When the puffins abandon their cliff-top burrows and head out to sea for the winter, this sheath falls off. The beak is then a much duller color until the following spring.

During display, these feathers are thrown open to produce a fountain of color as the male bird swings upside down from a branch

DANCING ON WATER
Great crested grebes perform a sequence of bizarre dances during their courtship. The sequence often begins with a head-shaking dance, in which the birds face each other, jerking their heads from side to side, as if trying to avoid each other's glance. Suddenly, they dive and reappear at the sur-face with beakfuls of water-weed. During the "penguin dance," both birds rear up out of the water, paddling furiously as they present the weed to each other. After several more dances, the birds mate.

MINIATURE RIVALS
Male hummingbirds, though tiny, aggress-ively defend their territories.

Camouflage

IN THE NATURAL WORLD, swaying reeds, beach pebbles, dead branches, and patches of snow are not always what they seem. Any one of them can suddenly burst into life to reveal its true identity - a bird that only moments before was perfectly camouflaged against its background. When faced with danger, most birds immediately take to the air. But some, especially those that feed or roost on the ground, prefer to take a chance that they will be overlooked. The birds that lie low the longest are those with camouflaged plumage. In these, the color and patterning of the feathers matches a particular kind of background, such as the forest floor.

Woodcock

HIDDEN AMONG THE PEBBLES
An open beach may seem a difficult place for a bird to conceal itself. But the moment it stops moving, a ringed plover vanishes among the beach pebbles.

Ringed plover

THE FIRST LINE OF DEFENSE
The woodcock is a forest bird that hunts mostly at night. Between dusk and dawn it probes the woodland floor for worms and other small animals, but during the day it roosts on the ground. If its camouflage fails to conceal it, the woodcock will take off and dash through the tree trunks with a swerving flight.

Probing beak

Seasonal changes

On high mountainsides, the winter snow completely changes the color of the landscape. Birds that do not fly south for the winter need some way to hide from their enemies. A few, like the rock ptarmigan (a type of grouse), do this by changing color. Because birds molt their feathers every year, they can change their color by shedding one set of feathers and replacing it with another, differently colored set. This enables them to camouflage themselves. In places where the snow never melts, birds like the snowy owl have white plumage all year long.

Rock ptarmigan in winter plumage

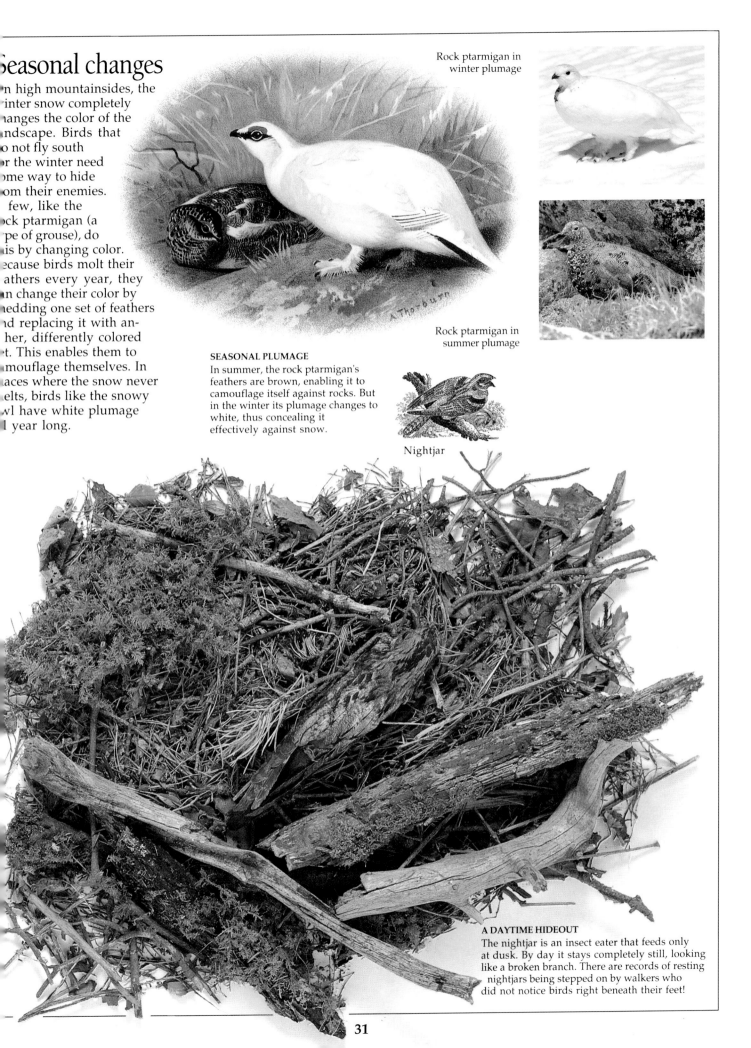

Rock ptarmigan in summer plumage

SEASONAL PLUMAGE
In summer, the rock ptarmigan's feathers are brown, enabling it to camouflage itself against rocks. But in the winter its plumage changes to white, thus concealing it effectively against snow.

Nightjar

A DAYTIME HIDEOUT
The nightjar is an insect eater that feeds only at dusk. By day it stays completely still, looking like a broken branch. There are records of resting nightjars being stepped on by walkers who did not notice birds right beneath their feet!

Feet and tracks

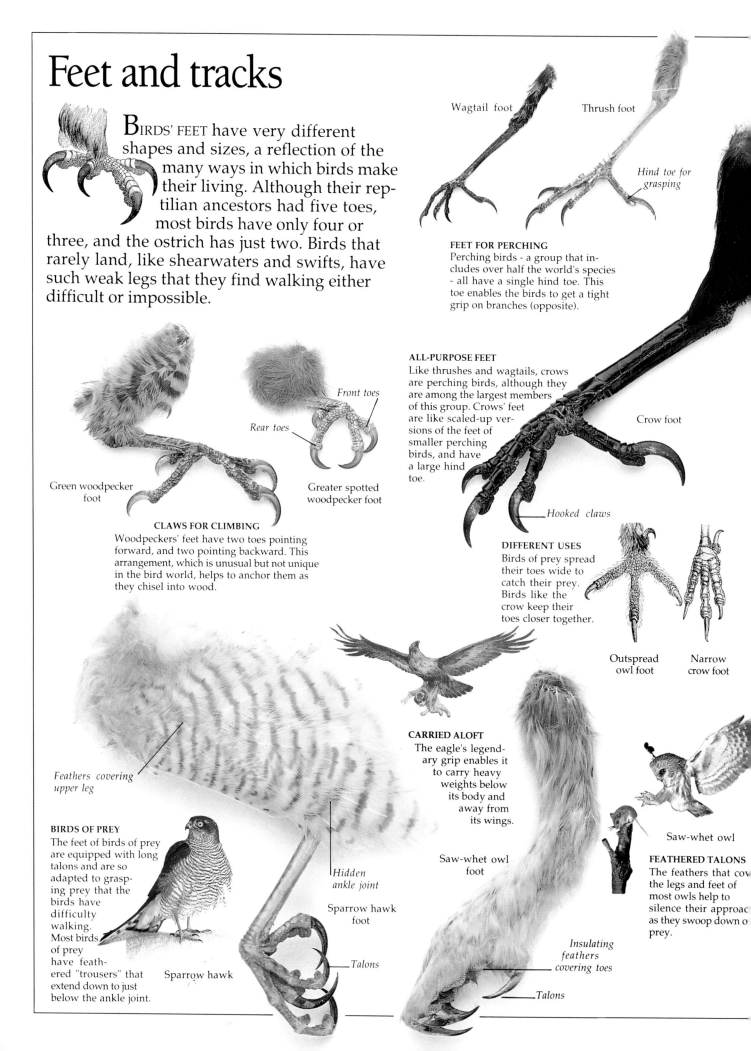

BIRDS' FEET have very different shapes and sizes, a reflection of the many ways in which birds make their living. Although their reptilian ancestors had five toes, most birds have only four or three, and the ostrich has just two. Birds that rarely land, like shearwaters and swifts, have such weak legs that they find walking either difficult or impossible.

Wagtail foot

Thrush foot

Hind toe for grasping

FEET FOR PERCHING
Perching birds - a group that includes over half the world's species - all have a single hind toe. This toe enables the birds to get a tight grip on branches (opposite).

ALL-PURPOSE FEET
Like thrushes and wagtails, crows are perching birds, although they are among the largest members of this group. Crows' feet are like scaled-up versions of the feet of smaller perching birds, and have a large hind toe.

Crow foot

Front toes

Rear toes

Greater spotted woodpecker foot

Green woodpecker foot

CLAWS FOR CLIMBING
Woodpeckers' feet have two toes pointing forward, and two pointing backward. This arrangement, which is unusual but not unique in the bird world, helps to anchor them as they chisel into wood.

Hooked claws

DIFFERENT USES
Birds of prey spread their toes wide to catch their prey. Birds like the crow keep their toes closer together.

Outspread owl foot

Narrow crow foot

CARRIED ALOFT
The eagle's legendary grip enables it to carry heavy weights below its body and away from its wings.

Feathers covering upper leg

BIRDS OF PREY
The feet of birds of prey are equipped with long talons and are so adapted to grasping prey that the birds have difficulty walking. Most birds of prey have feathered "trousers" that extend down to just below the ankle joint.

Sparrow hawk

Hidden ankle joint

Sparrow hawk foot

Talons

Saw-whet owl foot

Saw-whet owl

FEATHERED TALONS
The feathers that cover the legs and feet of most owls help to silence their approach as they swoop down on prey.

Insulating feathers covering toes

Talons

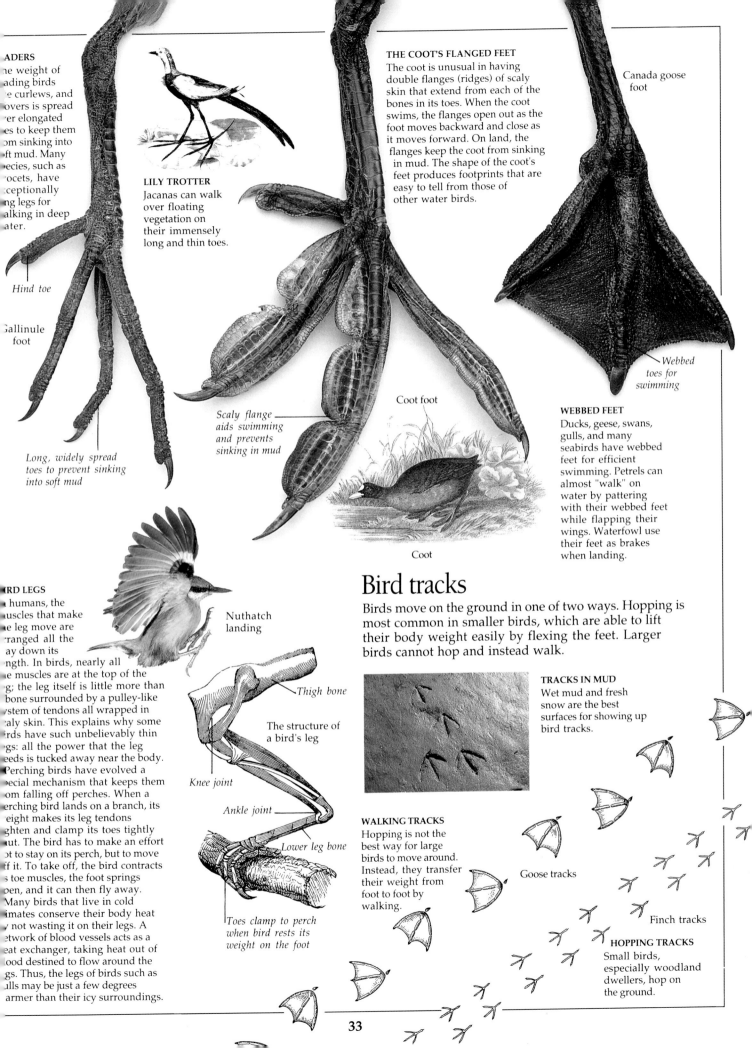

...e weight of
...ading birds
...e curlews, and
...overs is spread
...er elongated
...es to keep them
...om sinking into
...ft mud. Many
...ecies, such as
...ocets, have
...ceptionally
...ng legs for
...alking in deep
...ater.

Hind toe

...Gallinule
foot

*Long, widely spread
toes to prevent sinking
into soft mud*

LILY TROTTER
Jacanas can walk over floating vegetation on their immensely long and thin toes.

*Scaly flange
aids swimming
and prevents
sinking in mud*

THE COOT'S FLANGED FEET
The coot is unusual in having double flanges (ridges) of scaly skin that extend from each of the bones in its toes. When the coot swims, the flanges open out as the foot moves backward and close as it moves forward. On land, the flanges keep the coot from sinking in mud. The shape of the coot's feet produces footprints that are easy to tell from those of other water birds.

Coot foot

Coot

Canada goose foot

*Webbed
toes for
swimming*

WEBBED FEET
Ducks, geese, swans, gulls, and many seabirds have webbed feet for efficient swimming. Petrels can almost "walk" on water by pattering with their webbed feet while flapping their wings. Waterfowl use their feet as brakes when landing.

...RD LEGS
...humans, the
...uscles that make
...e leg move are
...ranged all the
...ay down its
...ngth. In birds, nearly all
...e muscles are at the top of the
...g; the leg itself is little more than
...bone surrounded by a pulley-like
...ystem of tendons all wrapped in
...aly skin. This explains why some
...rds have such unbelievably thin
...gs: all the power that the leg
...eeds is tucked away near the body.
...Perching birds have evolved a
...ecial mechanism that keeps them
...om falling off perches. When a
...erching bird lands on a branch, its
...eight makes its leg tendons
...ghten and clamp its toes tightly
...ut. The bird has to make an effort
...t to stay on its perch, but to move
...f it. To take off, the bird contracts
...s toe muscles, the foot springs
...pen, and it can then fly away.
...Many birds that live in cold
...imates conserve their body heat
...y not wasting it on their legs. A
...etwork of blood vessels acts as a
...eat exchanger, taking heat out of
...ood destined to flow around the
...gs. Thus, the legs of birds such as
...lls may be just a few degrees
...armer than their icy surroundings.

Nuthatch landing

Thigh bone

The structure of a bird's leg

Knee joint

Ankle joint

Lower leg bone

*Toes clamp to perch
when bird rests its
weight on the foot*

Bird tracks

Birds move on the ground in one of two ways. Hopping is most common in smaller birds, which are able to lift their body weight easily by flexing the feet. Larger birds cannot hop and instead walk.

TRACKS IN MUD
Wet mud and fresh snow are the best surfaces for showing up bird tracks.

WALKING TRACKS
Hopping is not the best way for large birds to move around. Instead, they transfer their weight from foot to foot by walking.

Goose tracks

Finch tracks

HOPPING TRACKS
Small birds, especially woodland dwellers, hop on the ground.

The senses

Birds live in a world that is dominated by sight and sound. Their sense of vision is so highly developed that for most birds, three of the other four senses - touch, smell, and taste - are largely irrelevant. A hovering kestrel sees very much greater detail on the ground below it than a human would at the same height, but at the same time, scientists are not sure if birds can taste their prey. Humans have thousands of taste buds on their tongues, most birds have fewer than a hundred. However, birds have good hearing. They can distinguish notes that are far too fast for humans to separate. One species, the oilbird of South America, can use sound to navigate just like a bat. But with skulls packed with such sensitive eyes and ears, birds have not evolved large brains.

Members of the crow family, such as the raven, are the acknowledged intellectuals of the bird world

Separate bones in the cranium are fused together into a light-weight, but strong, protective case

Cranium

Raven skull

Nostril cavity connects with small paired nostrils that lie just behind the horny sheath of the beak

Opening to internal ear, usually hidden by a thin layer of short feathers

Eye socket points sideways in nearly all birds except those that catch fast-moving prey such as mammals and fish

Jugal (cheek) bone at base of eye socket supports a bird's large eyes

SENSES AND THE SKULL
Like all parts of the raven's body, its skull is modified to make it light enough for flying. In most animals, the separate bony plates that make up the cranium meet at long joints called sutures. In a bird's cranium, the separate bones are fused together for extra strength, allowing the bones themselves to be thinner. The eyes are often bigger than the brain. They are kept in their sockets by a ring of tiny bones attached to the bird's eyeball.

INTELLIGENCE AND INSTINCT
Birds' brains are small compared to those of mammals, and most birds are poor at learning new skills. However, a bird is born with a huge number of "programs" built into its brain. These programs control not only simple activities like preening and feeding, but also feats of instinct such as migration.

Optic lobe

Cerebellum

Cerebral hemisphere

Spinal cord

The human's huge cerebral hemisphere allows rapid learning

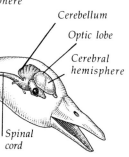

Cerebellum

Optic lobe

Cerebral hemisphere

Spinal cord

Much of the bird's brain is concerned with visual information

Cranium

Opposed eyes for wide-angle vision

Snipe skull

Bird vision

The eyes of owls point almost directly forward, giving them a wide field of binocular vision. This arrangement enables owls to judge distance very accurately, and it is shared by nearly all hunting birds. Birds that are themselves hunted tend to have eyes that point in opposite directions. The woodcock, for example, can see all around and above itself without moving its head. Most other birds' vision lies between these two extremes.

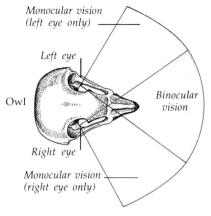

Monocular vision (left eye only)

Left eye

Owl

Binocular vision

Right eye

Monocular vision (right eye only)

REAR VIEW
Birds cannot swivel their eyeballs nearly as far as most other animals. An owl's eye movement, for example, is under two degrees, compared with 100 degrees for a human. Birds make up for this by having very flexible necks that can be turned to point backward.

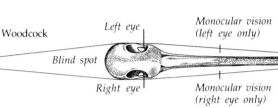

Woodcock

Left eye

Monocular vision (left eye only)

Forward binocular vision

Blind spot

Rear binocular vision field enables bird to see enemies approaching from behind

Right eye

Monocular vision (right eye only)

HUNTING IN DARKNESS
Some owls are able to hunt in complete darkness, using their ears to locate the sounds made by a scurrying animal.

Higher ear cavity

Lower ear cavity

The odd arrangement of an owl's ears is usually masked by its feathers

THE OWL'S UNBALANCED EARS
Owls hunt by night, when levels of light and sound are low. For this reason, an owl needs not only very acute vision but also extremely good hearing. Owls do not have external ears (although some species have earlike tufts of feathers). Instead their broad faces gather sound waves in the same way as an external ear and direct them to the eardrum within the skull. Owls' left and right ears are often at different levels in the skull. Each ear catches a sound at a slightly different time, giving improved "binaural" hearing which the owl uses to pinpoint its prey.

Hooked beak

Cranium

Forward-pointing eye socket for binocular vision

Ear

Owl skull

SENSITIVE BEAKS
Like other animals, birds feel with sensitive receptors that are attached to nerves. These receptors are scattered all over the body, but in long-billed birds they are also found on the tip of the beak. When a wading bird probes into deep mud with its beak, it can actually feel what is below it.

Snipe

Elongated upper and lower jawbones of beak enable the snipe to reach food buried in mud

Sensitive tip of beak detects buried animals

FEELING FOR FOOD
Nightjars have bristles that extend forward from each side of their mouths. These are extremely fine, barbless feathers, probably used to funnel flying insects into the bird's mouth. Although birds do not have sensory hairs such as whiskers, it is possible that the nightjar can use its bristles to feel food.

Beaks

BECAUSE THEIR FRONT LIMBS are completely adapted for flight, most birds - with the important exception of parrots and birds of prey - catch and hold their food with their beaks alone. Birds' beaks have evolved a great variety of specialized shapes to enable them to tackle different kinds of food. This specialization was shown until recently by the huia of New Zealand. In this remarkable species, sadly now extinct, the male's beak was short and straight for probing, and the female's was long and curved for picking out insects.

Cone-shaped beak   Chaffinch

THE SEED CRACKER
A bird's beak produces the greatest force nearest its base. Birds like chaffinches, which live on hard seeds, have short, cone-shaped beaks so that they can crack open their food with as much force as possible. Finches deftly remove the cases of seeds with their beaks before swallowing them.

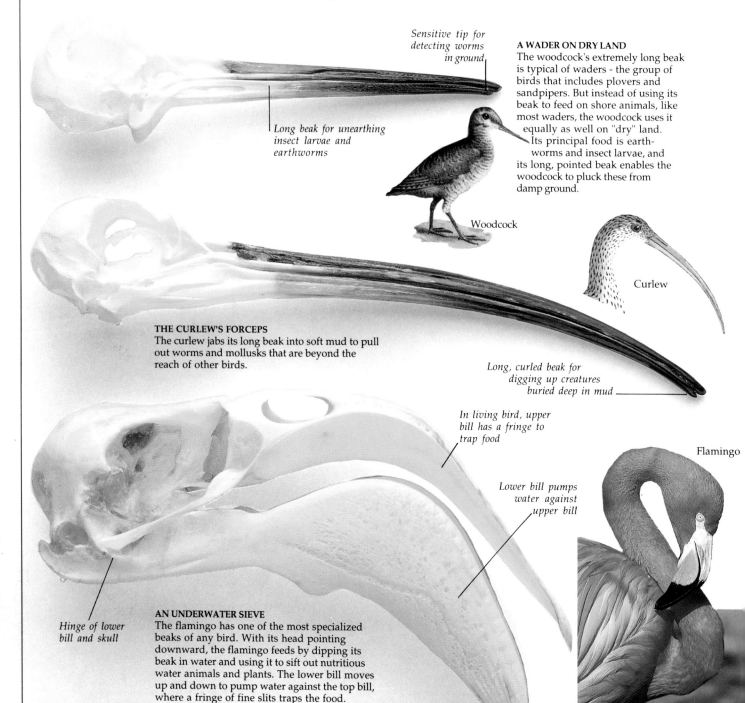

Sensitive tip for detecting worms in ground

Long beak for unearthing insect larvae and earthworms

A WADER ON DRY LAND
The woodcock's extremely long beak is typical of waders - the group of birds that includes plovers and sandpipers. But instead of using its beak to feed on shore animals, like most waders, the woodcock uses it equally as well on "dry" land. Its principal food is earthworms and insect larvae, and its long, pointed beak enables the woodcock to pluck these from damp ground.

Woodcock

Curlew

THE CURLEW'S FORCEPS
The curlew jabs its long beak into soft mud to pull out worms and mollusks that are beyond the reach of other birds.

Long, curled beak for digging up creatures buried deep in mud

In living bird, upper bill has a fringe to trap food

Lower bill pumps water against upper bill

Flamingo

Hinge of lower bill and skull

AN UNDERWATER SIEVE
The flamingo has one of the most specialized beaks of any bird. With its head pointing downward, the flamingo feeds by dipping its beak in water and using it to sift out nutritious water animals and plants. The lower bill moves up and down to pump water against the top bill, where a fringe of fine slits traps the food.

A MEAT-EATER'S BEAK
The kestrel has a hooked beak typical of falcons and other birds of prey. The hook enables these meat-eating birds to pull apart animals that are too big to be swallowed whole.

Hook

Kestrel

Medium-length pointed beak for seeds and larger food

European blackbird

A TWEEZER BEAK
The European blackbird has a beak shape that is shared by thousands of species of medium-size birds. It is sharply pointed to allow the bird to pick up small objects like seeds, but its length allows the bird to grasp larger food items such as earthworms. The male blackbird's orange-yellow beak is also used as a signal to female birds.

Parrot

Nostril

Area where seeds are cracked open

Hook for grasping fruit

A FRUIT-EATER'S BEAK
Wild parrots live on fruit and seeds and have a "combination" beak to allow them to make the most of their food. A parrot uses the hook at the beak's tip to pull at the pulp of fruit; it uses the jaws near the base of its beak to crack open seeds and reach the kernels. Parrots are unusual in the bird world in the way they also use their feet to hold and turn their food while they crack it open.

A BEAK FOR DABBLING
Many ducks feed by "dabbling," or opening and shutting the beak while skimming it across the water's surface. Water enters the two flattened halves of the beak, and anything in the water is strained out and swallowed. A duck's dabbling is rather like the sifting action of a flamingo, but a duck's beak is much less specialized and can be used for other kinds of feeding.

Teeth for catching fish, made out of the horny material of the beak

A DUCK WITH "TEETH"
Unlike mammals and reptiles, birds do not have true teeth that are made of bone. However, some birds have evolved structures that are very like teeth. The mergansers, for example, have tooth-like notches on the sides of their beaks. They use these beak teeth to catch fish, both in fresh water and out at sea.

Merganser

Flattened beak

Long, hooked beak for catching fish and ripping them apart

ALL-PURPOSE BEAK
Gulls' beaks are long and end in a hook that is smaller but in many ways similar to that of meat-eating birds. This beak shape not only enables a gull to catch and hold prey like fish along the length of the beak, but also allows them to pull apart their food.

Gull

Scoter

Plant and insect eaters

THE WORLD'S MOST NUMEROUS wild bird, the red-billed quelea, is a seed eater. Over one hundred billion of these birds scour African fields and grassland for food, forming flocks that are millions strong. Birds like the quelea can survive in huge numbers because they live on a food that is incredibly abundant. Seeds, grass, nectar, insects, worms, and many other small animals exist in vast amounts, and together they form the food for the majority of the world's birds.

Thrush

Eating plants and seeds

Birds that eat plants and seeds have to crush their food before they can digest it. As they have no teeth, they do this with powerful beaks and also with the gizzard (p. 8) - a muscular "grinding chamber" in their stomachs.

Finch skull

Hard-cased seeds

SPECIALIST SEED EATERS
Finches, which number over 150 species, have short, sharp bills for breaking open seeds and nuts. Amazingly, some finches have bills that can exert more crushing force than a human hand.

Goose skull

Leaf crops

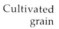

Pigeon skull

FEEDING ON CROPS
Pigeons and doves originally ate the leaves and seeds of wild plants; now they often feed on cultivated ones as well. They can also use their pointed bills like a straw when drinking - a unique ability among birds.

Cultivated grain

LIVING ON GRASS
Geese are among the few kinds of birds that can live on a diet of grass. But geese digest grass poorly, and it passes through their bodies in just two hours. Because they get so little out of their food, they must eat a lot of it and so feed almost constantly.

Broad bill for tearing grass

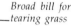

Capercaillie skull

Powerful hooked beak for grasping leaves from trees and crushing seeds

ALL-AROUND PLANT EATERS
Game birds - species like pheasants, grouse, and this capercaillie from northern Europe - eat whatever plant food is available, although their preference is for seeds. In winter, the capercaillie lives on the leaves of cone-bearing trees, a source of food that few other animals use. It pulls the leaves from branches with its powerful hooked beak

Seeds

Needles of cone-bearing trees

The grass and water plants on which geese feed

Invertebrate eaters

Every spring, the number of insects and other invertebrates (animals without backbones) increases dramatically. These animals form the food for dozens of species of migratory birds. In winter, the supply is much smaller and food is harder to find, consisting mainly of larvae (grubs) in wood or in the soil. These are sought out by specialist insect eaters.

Blackcap skull

Aphids

Caterpillar

PROBING WARBLERS

These small songsters use their delicate probing beaks to pick insects from leaves and bark. When the supply dries up in early autumn, they migrate south.

THE SNAIL SMASHER

Thrushes eat a wide range of food, both plant and animal. Some feed on snails, which they smash open on stone "anvils."

Thrush skull

Snail shells broken open by thrush

Earthworms are eaten not only by garden birds, but also by some owls and even birds of prey

Pecked apple

Woodpecker skull

Centipede

Beetle larvae

Adult beetle

LARGE INSECT EATERS

Birds like woodpeckers and the mainly ground-feeding hoopoe use their beaks to pick large insects out of crevices in trees. Woodpeckers also chisel into the wood to find concealed grubs. Their extremely long tongues have spearlike tips that are used for stabbing their prey.

Hoopoe skull

Avocet feeding

Ribbon worm

Silt-burrowing lugworm

Feeding on the shore

Although there are very few salt-water insects, the seashore contains a year-round supply of other invertebrates for birds to eat, from crabs and shellfish to burrowing worms.

Avocet skull

THE SWEEP-NET BEAK

The avocet catches worms and other prey by striding forward and sweeping its beak from side to side. It is one of the very few birds with an upturned beak.

Worms

Crab broken open and eaten; the hard skeleton is usually discarded

Oyster catcher skull

Mussel

A BUILT-IN HAMMER

The oyster catcher feeds on seashore animals with hard shells. It has a long beak like the avocet, but instead of ending in a fine point, its tip is blunt. This built-in "hammer" enables the oyster catcher to smash through the shells of its prey. Such feeding needs a great deal of skill, and some oyster catchers prize shells open instead. An experienced bird will know precisely where the weak points are on a mussel or cockleshell, and if the shell is lying on sand, the bird will carry it to a rock to break it open.

Cockles

Hunters, fishers, and all-arounders

FLIGHT ENABLES BIRDS to cover great distances in search of food. This gives them a big advantage as predators, because few animals - on land or far out at sea - are beyond their reach. Flight also makes birds very effective all-around feeders. A dead animal, an unprotected nest, or a field of ripening crops is quickly spotted by passing birds and turned into a satisfying meal.

Kingfishers

Strips of meat torn from prey with powerful hooked beak

Tawny owl skull

Fur is swallowed and later discarded in pellets

Meat and fish eaters

Birds that feed on larger animals and fish catch their prey in two different ways. Most fish eaters use their beaks to catch their quarry. On land, birds of prey use their talons for catching and their beaks for tearing.

Buzzard skull

NIGHT AND DAY HUNTERS
In general, owls and birds of prey such as the buzzard operate like two sets of shift workers, catching rodents and larger mammals around the clock. A few owls do hunt by day, but no bird of prey can hunt during the night because their eyesight and hearing is not good enough.

Large forward-pointing eyes enable the gannet to pinpoint fish below

Halves of the beak meet at a long straight line for holding fish before they are swallowed

Streamlined point for diving

ABOVE AND BELOW WATER
Gannets dive-bomb shoals of fish by plunging, with their wings folded, from heights of up to 100 ft (30 m). They stay below the surface for only a few seconds. Cormorants pursue fish underwater. Their feathers do not trap air like those of other water birds, and this enables them to dive swiftly and overtake their prey.

Gannet skull

PATIENCE REWARDED
The heron fishes by stealth, staying motionless until its prey swims within reach of its long stabbing beak.

Hooked beak for grasping fish

Cormorant skull

Mackerel

A mixed diet

It doesn't take much intelligence to be a successful seed eater, but birds that survive on a mixed diet must live by their wits. These scavengers are quick to take a chance that might lead to a meal; other birds would hesitate and miss out. They thrive on waste food and household rubbish, as well as more natural food items.

Crows eat all kinds of animal remains and are particularly skilled at finding animal casualties on roads

Seeds from fields and farmyards

ETAL MEALS

striches are famed for eir scavenging. They ve even been known eat metal, sometimes ith fatal results.

Magpie skull

Ground beetle

Centipede

Insects and invertebrates, usually swallowed whole and partially regurgitated in pellets (p. 42)

(p. 42)

Egg broken open after being stolen from nest

row skull

Jay skull

Earthworm

Nuts eaten by birds have rough-edged holes; those eaten by rodents show small teeth marks

EVER-ADAPTABLE CROWS

The members of the crow family are among the most successful general feeders in the bird world. There are few places where they cannot be found. One of the reasons for their success is their curious nature, which is backed up by boldness and a strong, all-purpose beak. Insects, dead birds, live mammals, worms, and seeds all feature on their menu, and anything that cannot be eaten may well be carried off for further inspection.

Broad-bodied
libellula
dragonfly larva

Toad tadpole

Duckweed

Ramsnorn
water snail

Greater
pondsnail

Coot skul

A FRESHWATER OPPORTUNIST

The coot is a small, aggressive bird of lakes and rivers. It eats any water life that it can find - including not only waterweeds, snails, tadpoles, and fish but also young birds. Young ducklings are particularly at risk from the coot's attacks.

Algae

Water snails from slow-moving fresh water

Animals and plants eaten by coots in shallow ponds

Pellets

PREDATORY BIRDS like owls feed on small mammals and birds, but because they do not have teeth, they cannot chew their food. Instead, they either rip their prey apart with their claws or eat it whole. This means that they swallow large quantities of bones, fur, and feathers, which they cannot digest. So once or twice a day they regurgitate (expel through the mouth) these items, packed tightly together, as pellets. The shape of a pellet identifies the species of bird that produced it, and the contents of the pellet show what the bird has been eating.

PELLETS IN OPEN GROUND
The short-eared owl hunts in daylight over rough grassland and marshes, catching voles and sometimes young birds. Its pellets are long, with rounded ends. This particular species of owl does not drop its pellets from a perch but scatters them around low clumps of grass.

Rounded ends

Limb bone from a rodent

Blunt ends

Smooth dark crust

PELLETS BENEATH A ROOST
The smooth, almost black pellets of the barn owl are easy to identify. They often accumulate in small piles beneath roosts in old barns and other buildings.

Recent pellet still in compact state

Older pellet beginning to disintegrate

Pointed ends

Protruding bones, typical of tawny owl pellets

Beetle wing case

Earth and fur

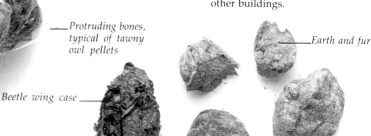

PELLETS IN PARKS AND GARDENS
Tawny owl pellets are the only ones commonly found in parks - where the owl often nests - in suburbs, and also in the countryside. Tawny owls eat voles, mice, shrews, and birds, as well as much smaller animals. Their pellets are smooth and sometimes have pointed ends. Pellets that have been on the ground for a while often crumble to reveal a mass of protruding bones and tangled fur.

A VARIED DIET
All these pellets are from little owls. They show how a bird's diet can change the appearance of its pellets. The smaller pellets contain fur and earth - the earth having been produced by a meal of earthworms. The larger pellets also contain earth and small amounts of fur, but packed into this are the legs and wing cases of beetles.

Beetle leg

Shell fragments

Seed cases mixed with pieces of shell

WADER PELLETS
The curlew and many other wading birds eat hard-shelled animals such as crabs. Their pellets contain pieces of these shells, sometimes mixed with the cases of seeds.

Wing cases of beetles mixed in with plant material

CROW PELLETS
Crows and their relatives eat all kinds of food. Their pellets often contain insect remains and plant stalks.

Seeds left behind after the soft flesh of berries has been digested

Tin foil

SONGBIRD PELLETS
Thrushes and blackbirds produce pellets that contain seeds. This specimen also contains a small piece of tin foil.

Rodent limb bone

Fur

FALCON PELLETS
Birds like the kestrel and peregrine falcon produce pellets that contain bird, mammal, and insect remains.

nside an owl pellet

y pulling apart a pellet, it is ossible to find out something about an wl's diet. Here two tawny owl ellets have been carefully taken part. The first pellet shows that the wl that produced it had dined ntirely on voles - three of these small ammals made up the bird's nightly atch. The second pellet tells a rather ifferent and more surprising story.

COMPLETE PELLET
When the pellet is dry, the fur and bones are matted together.

Fur, mixed with mucus, forms the "glue" that binds the pellet together

Rodents can be identified by the shape of their cheek teeth; these are from a vole

Ball joint on leg bone fits into this socket

Three vole skulls, two still intact

heek teeth

Complete jaw

Incisors

The two sides of the jaw often break apart in the owl's stomach and they usually become separated from the skull

Hip bones with sockets for the back leg joint

Bones from front limbs

Shoulder blades, which attach to the front legs

Leg bones, some still paired as they would have been in life

Curved ribs with flattened sides

Vertebrae - the distinctive bones that make up the backbone

EEDING ON OTHER BIRDS

lthough owls are often thought of as living on dents and nothing else, these starling bones ow that birds are very much a feature of the wny owl's diet. Amazingly, the owl has man- ;ed to swallow and regurgitate the starling's rge skull almost intact. Feathers, like fur and aws, are made of an indigestible protein, and ve to be disposed of along with the bones.

Starling skull

Lower half of beak

Vertebrae from the starling's backbone

Wishbone (part of the shoulder)

Leg with complete claw still attached

Foot

Claw

Swallowed body feathers

Flight feathers - quills of some have snapped in two

Leg and wing bones

Ribs

Making a nest

NEST BUILDING is a job with two parts that are done at the same time: collecting the materials and fashioning them into the finished nest. The amount of time spent collecting depends on how far away the materials are: a reed warbler hardly has to move to find dry reed leaves, but a swallow must find a puddle that will provide exactly the kind of mud it needs. Birds go through a special series of movements to work materials into their nests. When a cup nester returns to the nest with materials, it first pushes them roughly into place. The bird then sits in the center of the nest and begins to turn around and around, pushing downward and outward with its breast. This circular movement, which gives the inside of the nest its shape, is shared by all birds. Cup nesters turn and push; birds such as herons turn and trample, pulling at individual sticks on the nest platform as they do so.

NATURAL MATERIALS
Nest materials have two main functions: support and insulation. Most hedgerow and woodland birds use sticks for the main structure of their nests, then add an insulating lining which may be of feathers, seed heads, or animal fur. House martins and some swallows make their nests entirely out of mud. Another insect eater, the swift, collects nesting material in midair by catching floating fibers in its beak.

MUD
Mixed with saliva to form a sticky paste.

SEED HEADS
Used in the nest lining for insulation.

LEAVES AND NEEDLES
Used for the inside of many cup nests.

TWIGS AND STICKS
Main structural material in larger nests.

MAN-MADE MATERIALS
Anything that can be carried away may end up in a bird's nest. Pigeons have been found nesting, quite literally, on beds of nails, and coots on plastic bags. Storks may use old clothes and other rubbish to build their massive nests.

Hooded crow

STRING
Small lengths are found in many nests.

TIN FOIL
Often collected by crows and magpies.

PLASTIC BALER TWINE
A favorite with birds nesting on farmland.

PAPER AND TISSUE
Found in the nests of many city birds.

Nest ingredients

Packed with a huge variety of ingredients, the pied wagtail's nest shown here is like a guide to a complete habitat. Its owner has scoured fields, hedgerows, old walls, and fences for plant and animal materials, making hundreds or perhaps thousands of trips to bring all that it has collected back to the growing nest.

FEATHERS
These are collected from the ground, sometimes around fox kills, and from old nests.

MEDLEY OF MATERIALS
Small nests usually have the widest variety of materials.

Body and down feathers for insulation

Fur and hair for insulation

CATTLE HAIR
Like wool, this good insulator is collected from fences and thorny bushes.

WOOL
Tufts caught on barbed wire are removed by many nesting birds.

Dry grass seed heads to form structure

MOSS
Moss traps air and prevents heat loss - essential for the protection of young nestlings.

Moss for insulation

Lichens for camouflage

LICHENS
Lichens pulled from stone walls and tree branches may help to camouflage the nest.

HORSE HAIR
Coarse hair from a horse's tail helps to form the nest's cup shape.

GRASS
Leaves and seed heads are worked into the nest's structure.

45

Cup nests

BIRD NESTS COME IN ALL SHAPES AND SIZES. They can be tiny shelves of saliva that are glued to the walls of caves, long tunnels that run many yards into the ground, or, in the case of some eagles, massive piles of branches that weigh more than a family-size car. But the most familiar nests are undoubtedly the cup nests, which are built by birds of woodland, hedgerows, and farmland. Despite their overall similarity, the fine details of these nests identify their makers as surely as a fingerprint.

Rooks nesting on a weathervane

Chaffinch at nest

Moss and lichen cup forms the main structure of the nest

Feathers from other birds provide insulation

Dried moss

Hair and feather lining insulates the eggs and developing nestlings

Redstart

SPIDERWEB FOUNDATIONS

To make its nest, a chaffinch first loops strands of spiders' webs around a group of forked branches. These are the anchors for the nest; once they are secure, the bird builds up the cup with moss, lichens, and grass, then lines it with feathers and hair. Collecting these nesting materials takes a long time. If for any reason the chaffinch decides that its nest site is unsafe, it will transfer materials from the old nest to a new site to avoid too much extra work.

SECONDHAND FEATHERED LINING

Feathers are an important part of many birds' nests. Songbirds like the redstart, whose nest is shown here, collect feathers shed by other birds. Water fowl and waders use their own feathers. Some small birds, such as sparrows, improve on the natural supply by pulling feathers from the backs of larger birds.

Mud lining

Song thrush feeding young

Outer cup

MASTERPIECE IN MUD

Many cup-nest builders use mud to make their nests, in most cases applying it as a layer just beneath a final lining of feathers, hair, or grass. The song thrush is unusual in choosing mud as the lining itself. The bird makes a strong outer cup of twigs and grass, and then it smears the semi-liquid lining around the inside. Although mud makes up most of the mixture, it also contains saliva and animal droppings. Once the lining has been applied, it becomes hard. Even after the birds have left the nest it can withstand rain for many months.

Nests on buildings

Although it has taken birds millions of years to develop their nest-building skills, they are surprisingly quick to make use of any new sites that become available. Stone and brick houses are a relatively recent feature on the Earth. However, in the few thousand years that buildings have been around, some birds, especially house martins, swifts, swallows, and storks, have taken up residence on them in large numbers. Walls and window ledges make an ideal home for cliffs-nesting birds; rooftops and chimneys are used by birds that originally nested in treetops; and kettles, shelves and tool sheds are used by hedgerow species.

TREE SUBSTITUTE
Storks pile up their stick nests on chimneys and the tops of buildings. A pair of storks returns to the same site year after year.

ARTIFICIAL CLIFFS
Swallows and martins glue their mud nests onto ledges and vertical walls.

HEDGEROW HEIGHT
Hedge birds pick sites by height. This broom is right for a blackbird.

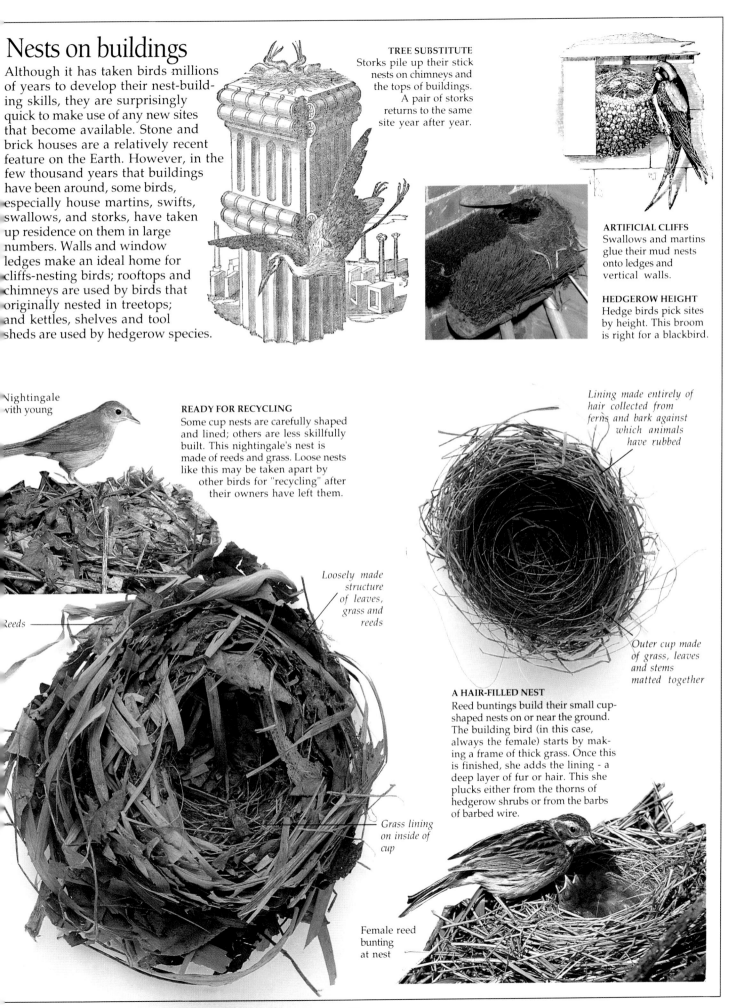

Nightingale with young

READY FOR RECYCLING
Some cup nests are carefully shaped and lined; others are less skillfully built. This nightingale's nest is made of reeds and grass. Loose nests like this may be taken apart by other birds for "recycling" after their owners have left them.

Lining made entirely of hair collected from ferns and bark against which animals have rubbed

Loosely made structure of leaves, grass and reeds

Reeds

Outer cup made of grass, leaves and stems matted together

A HAIR-FILLED NEST
Reed buntings build their small cup-shaped nests on or near the ground. The building bird (in this case, always the female) starts by making a frame of thick grass. Once this is finished, she adds the lining - a deep layer of fur or hair. This she plucks either from the thorns of hedgerow shrubs or from the barbs of barbed wire.

Grass lining on inside of cup

Female reed bunting at nest

47

Unusual nests

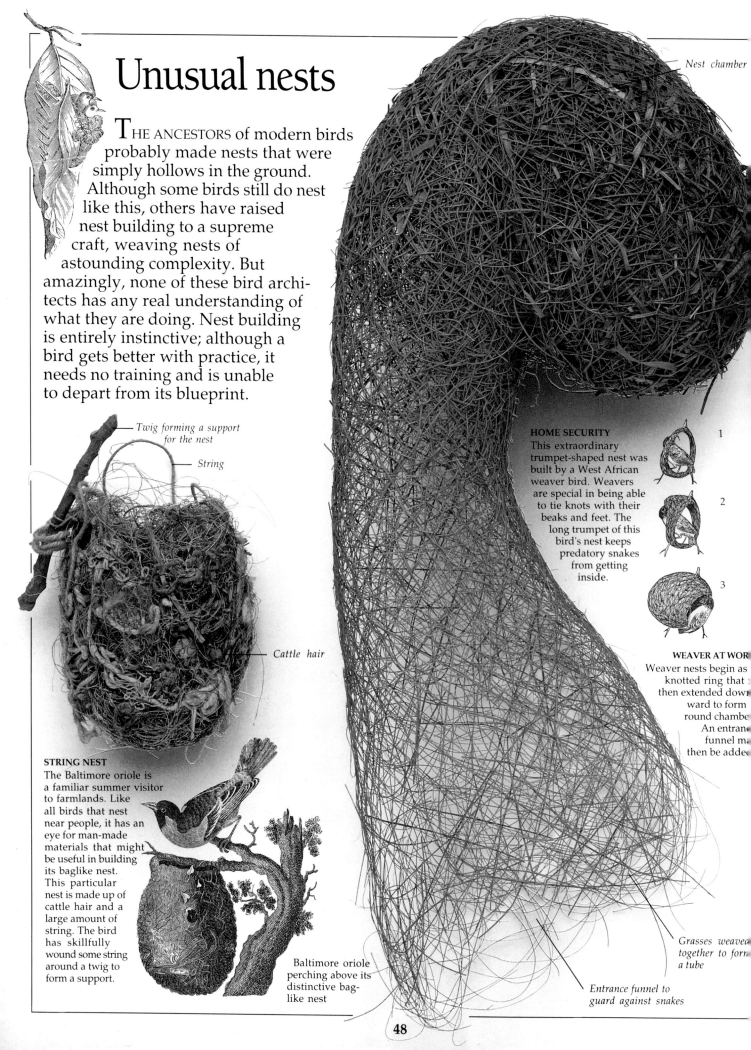

THE ANCESTORS of modern birds probably made nests that were simply hollows in the ground. Although some birds still do nest like this, others have raised nest building to a supreme craft, weaving nests of astounding complexity. But amazingly, none of these bird architects has any real understanding of what they are doing. Nest building is entirely instinctive; although a bird gets better with practice, it needs no training and is unable to depart from its blueprint.

Twig forming a support for the nest

String

Cattle hair

STRING NEST
The Baltimore oriole is a familiar summer visitor to farmlands. Like all birds that nest near people, it has an eye for man-made materials that might be useful in building its baglike nest. This particular nest is made up of cattle hair and a large amount of string. The bird has skillfully wound some string around a twig to form a support.

Baltimore oriole perching above its distinctive bag-like nest

Nest chamber

HOME SECURITY
This extraordinary trumpet-shaped nest was built by a West African weaver bird. Weavers are special in being able to tie knots with their beaks and feet. The long trumpet of this bird's nest keeps predatory snakes from getting inside.

1

2

3

WEAVER AT WORK
Weaver nests begin as a knotted ring that is then extended downward to form a round chamber. An entrance funnel may then be added.

Grasses weaved together to form a tube

Entrance funnel to guard against snakes

48

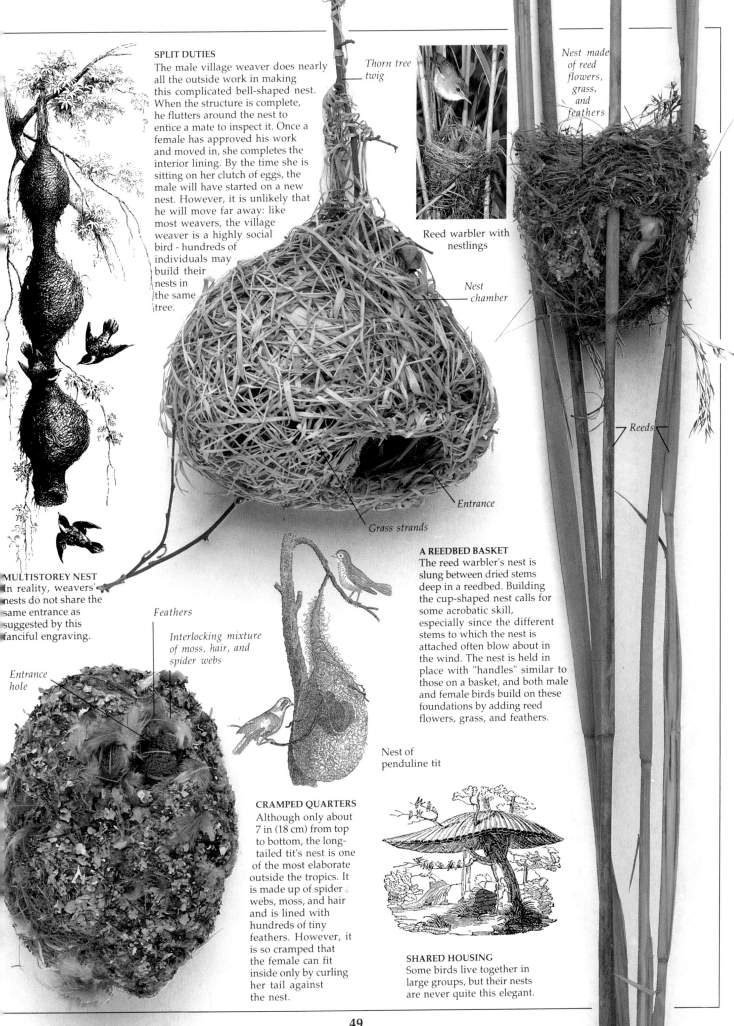

SPLIT DUTIES
The male village weaver does nearly all the outside work in making this complicated bell-shaped nest. When the structure is complete, he flutters around the nest to entice a mate to inspect it. Once a female has approved his work and moved in, she completes the interior lining. By the time she is sitting on her clutch of eggs, the male will have started on a new nest. However, it is unlikely that he will move far away: like most weavers, the village weaver is a highly social bird - hundreds of individuals may build their nests in the same tree.

Thorn tree twig

Nest chamber

Reed warbler with nestlings

Nest made of reed flowers, grass, and feathers

Reeds

Entrance

Grass strands

MULTISTOREY NEST
In reality, weavers' nests do not share the same entrance as suggested by this fanciful engraving.

Feathers

Interlocking mixture of moss, hair, and spider webs

Entrance hole

A REEDBED BASKET
The reed warbler's nest is slung between dried stems deep in a reedbed. Building the cup-shaped nest calls for some acrobatic skill, especially since the different stems to which the nest is attached often blow about in the wind. The nest is held in place with "handles" similar to those on a basket, and both male and female birds build on these foundations by adding reed flowers, grass, and feathers.

Nest of penduline tit

CRAMPED QUARTERS
Although only about 7 in (18 cm) from top to bottom, the long-tailed tit's nest is one of the most elaborate outside the tropics. It is made up of spider webs, moss, and hair and is lined with hundreds of tiny feathers. However, it is so cramped that the female can fit inside only by curling her tail against the nest.

SHARED HOUSING
Some birds live together in large groups, but their nests are never quite this elegant.

Eggs of water birds and waders

THE KIND OF EGG that a bird lays depends on how it lives. True seabirds (ones that come ashore only to breed) usually lay a single egg on rocky ledges away from enemies. Wading birds lay more eggs, but on the coasts and inlets there is little cover for their nests, so their eggs are camouflaged.

Gulls

FOSTERED EGGS
A gallinule may sneak the first of its clutch of eggs into another bird's nest for the unsuspecting neighbor to look after. After this, the gallinule settles down to raise up to a dozen of its own eggs itself.

 WARNING All the eggs shown here come from established museum collections. Collecting or handling wild birds' eggs is now illegal.

Shoveler duck

Undersize egg

A TERN'S EGGS
Least terns lay two or three eggs at a time in a hollow in the ground, usually in a pile of pebbles. The eggs' delicate patterning makes them almost impossible to see against the surrounding pebbles.

Normal egg

VARIATIONS IN SIZE
Just as a litter of mammals may contain an undersize specimen, so occasionally may a clutch of eggs. These two eggs are both from a shoveler duck. Like most ducks, it produces a large number of eggs - between eight and 12 in a nest.

EGGS UNDER GUARD
Common tern eggs are fearlessly defended by their parents. During incubation, the birds attack any intruder - even humans - by diving directly at them.

GULL EGGS
Many gulls lay their eggs on the ground, where camouflage is important. This egg is from one of the largest gulls, the great black-backed gull. Its speckled color hides it from predators, which can include other gulls, during the four weeks it takes to hatch.

THE EGG THAT ROLLS BACK
The murre produces one of the most unusually shaped and differently colored eggs of all birds. Murres do not build nests. Instead, each female lays its single egg directly on a bare cliff ledge. The egg's pointed shape helps to keep her from accidentally knocking it off its risky spot. Should it begin to roll, it will travel back in a circle rather than on in a straight line. The different colors are more difficult to explain. They may help parents to recognize their own egg among the thousands in a murre colony.

Murre

Cream and brown form

White form

Streaked gray form

50

AMOUFLAGE AND CONFUSION

e little ringed plover lays its
gs on gravel and pebbles near
ter, where the eggs are protected
their camouflage coloring. If an
ruder approaches the nest, the
rent birds often fly directly at it,
ward the source of danger, veering
ay at the last minute in an
empt to distract attention from
eggs. When the eggs have
tched, this distraction display
comes even more complicated,
th the parents scuttling away
m the nestlings to confuse
emies.

SLOW DEVELOPER

The fulmar's single egg needs a long
seven and a half weeks of incubation before it will hatch. The egg
is laid on a cliff ledge. Its color
shows that there is little need for
camouflage so far beyond the reach
of land predators.

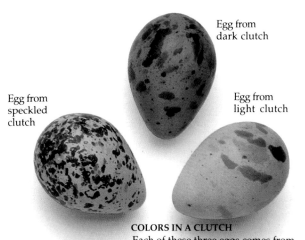

Egg from
speckled
clutch

Egg from
dark clutch

Egg from
light clutch

COLORS IN A CLUTCH

Each of these three eggs comes from
a small wading bird. Many
camouflaged eggs vary
widely in both pattern and
color between clutches. However,
within a single clutch the eggs are
much more closely matched.

Snipe

THE DOUBLE-POINTED EGG

The great crested grebe
lays its curiously
shaped eggs on a mound
of waterlogged veg-
etation. Most grebes
have unusually pointed
eggs, but no one knows why.

Curlew

HEAVYWEIGHT WADER

Pointed at one end and blunt at the
other, the curlew's egg is easy to
identify. Like most
waders, the curlew
lays its clutch in a
"scrape" on the ground.

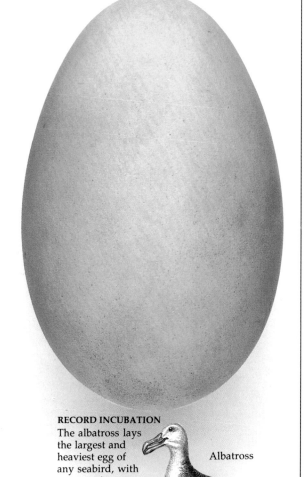

RECORD INCUBATION

The albatross lays
the largest and
heaviest egg of
any seabird, with
some specimens
weighing more than
1.1 lb (500 g). Albatross
eggs have the longest
incubation period
of any bird: parents
sit on a single egg for
two and a half months.

Albatross

ONCEALED IN THE TREETOPS

e gray heron builds its nest high
the trees, so its blue eggs are
rely seen in one piece. When
sh, this egg was bright blue, but
e color has faded over the years.

AT THE WATER'S EDGE

Loons are freshwater fish-eating
birds. They are clumsy on land, so
they lay their dark brown eggs
right by the water's edge to reduce
the risk of damage.

Eggs of land birds

SMALL LAND BIRDS, like the seed and insect eaters, lay small eggs. However, many produce large clutches - sometimes well over a dozen eggs. Others get through their breeding cycle very quickly and cram a number of clutches into a single season. Large birds, on the other hand, lay far fewer eggs. For birds such as eagles and vultures, one small clutch a year is all they produce.

Some of the specimens shown have lost the brightness of their original colors due to age

Tawny owl egg

Little owl egg

DOWN ON THE GROUND
Buntings are sparrow-like birds that lay their eggs on or near the ground. This is the egg of a corn bunting, a species unusual in that up to seven females may share the same mate.

HIGHLY VISIBLE EGGS
Owl eggs are white, almost round, and have a glossy surface. The round shape is typical of many eggs laid in holes. They might be white so the parent bird can see them, or the color may have evolved because there is no need for camouflage.

Long-eared owl

THE CHIMNEY NESTER
The jackdaw, a member of the crow family, lays its eggs in holes, either in trees, rocky outcrops, or buildings. Chimneys are one of its favorite nesting sites - sometimes with disastrous results.

HIDDEN IN THE UNDERGROWTH
The nightingale makes its nest in low, tangled bushes. Its brown eggs are well hidden in the shadows cast by leaves and branches.

Wood warbler egg   Marsh warbler egg

SUMMER VISITORS
Most of the world's 400 species of warbler migrate to breed. They arrive at the same time as the annual insect population explosion, which provides food for the average family of six nestlings.

ADDED COLOR
Surface colors like the brown and gray streaks on this Baltimore oriole's egg are formed just a few hours before the egg is laid.

Baltimore oriole

Normal egg   Outsize egg

ABNORMAL EGGS
During the process of egg production, things sometimes go wrong. A single egg may have two yolks, or it may be of a different size to a normal egg. The eggs shown here are crow's eggs.

Carrion crow

Coal tit egg

Blue tit egg

HEAVYWEIGHT CLUTCH
Tits, including the coal tit, blue tit, and American chickadee, lay up to 15 eggs, each clutch weighing up to a third more than the bird.

Chaffinch egg   Hawfinch egg

SLOW BEGINNERS
Finches lay betweeen four and six eggs in trees and bushes. Some finches do not lay eggs until early summer when seeds, their staple food, become available.

LESS TO LAY
The wood pigeon, a typical medium-size bird, lays two eggs. Together they weigh less than a tenth of the parent - a tiny proportion compared to the eggs of smaller birds.

MOORLAND CAMOUFLAGE
One look at a grouse's camouflaged egg shows that this bird nests on the ground. Dark blotches help to conceal clutches of up to ten eggs during the month-long incubation among heather and bracken.

52

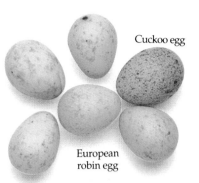

Cuckoo egg

Dunnock egg

Cuckoo egg

European robin egg

THE CUCKOO'S DECEPTION
Cuckoos lay their eggs in the nests of other birds. The host birds are always much smaller than the cuckoo, and during the course of time, the cuckoo has evolved eggs that are tiny for a bird of its size. Here a cuckoo has laid an egg among a robin's clutch.

Cuckoo

A POOR MATCH
The European cuckoo has too many hosts to match all their eggs.

AMERICAN ROBIN
This bird is a member of the thrush family, unlike the European robin.

NONSTOP PRODUCTION
The European blackbird's clutch of four eggs is typical of members of the thrush family. They all have the ability to raise more than one family in a year. If conditions are especially good, a female blackbird can lay up to five clutches in a season. However, winter takes its toll on many of the offspring, and few survive into the following year.

DAYTIME DISGUISE
The nocturnal nightjar does not make a nest. Instead, it lays its pair of eggs on rough ground. The eggs' camouflage is almost as good as the parent bird's (p. 30).

HOLE NESTER
Many woodpeckers chisel out nest holes in trees. Their eggs are very similar to those of hole-nesting owls - white and glossy.

RAISED AMONG THE ROOFTOPS
The kestrel lays a clutch of four to six eggs. It occasionally nests on city buildings, where its eggs perch at great risk on gutters and window ledges.

VULNERABLE HAWKS
The sparrowhawk is currently recovering from damage caused by DDT. Although bright blue when laid, sparrowhawk eggs gradually fade.

FISH-EATING FALCON
The osprey - one of the most widely distributed birds in the world - has eggs of highly variable color. They take about five weeks to be incubated.

OLD WORLD VULTURE
The Egyptian vulture lays its eggs high up on cliffs and in cave mouths. As an adult, it feeds on the eggs of other large birds, smashing them open with a stone.

ONE OF A PAIR
Eagles lay eggs in clutches of two. Unlike small birds, which lay an egg a day, eagles leave an interval of several days between laying the first and second egg.

SLOW DEVELOPERS
Buzzards lay between two and four eggs in a clutch. Incubation takes over five weeks and the nestlings stay in the nest for another six weeks. As a result, parents can raise only one clutch a year.

Extraordinary eggs

THE LARGEST living bird, the ostrich, lays an egg that is 4,500 times heavier than that of the smallest, a hummingbird. But going back in time, one of the heaviest birds that ever existed - the elephant bird - laid eggs that could each have swallowed up seven ostrich eggs with room to spare. The extraordinary differences in sizes of bird species is demonstrated especially vividly by their eggs.

THE ROC
This creature from th[e] *Arabian Nights* may have actually existe[d] not as an inhabitant [of] the air, but as the hu[ge] and flightless eleph[ant] bird of Madagascar.

HUMMINGBIRD EGG
Each egg weighs about one fifth of the adult's weight.

OSTRICH EGG
Each egg weigh[s] up to 3.3 lb (1.5 kg) - ab[out] one hundre[dth] of the adult's weigh[t.]

Hummingbirds

LIGHTER THAN FEATHERS
Hummingbirds lay the smallest eggs of any bird. The very tiniest of them measures about 0.4 in (1 cm) from end to end and weighs about 0.01 oz (0.35 g). Hummingbird eggs are long with rounded edges, and only two are laid in the tiny, cup-shaped nest. It takes about three weeks for the nestlings to grow all their feathers and leave the nest to fend for themselves.

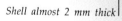

Shell almost 2 mm thick

CLUBBING TOGETHER
The ostrich lays the largest egg of any bird alive today. Although a single hen lays a clutch of about 10, more than one bird may lay in the same place, helping to create an unmanageable pile of perhaps as many as 50 eggs.

Ostrich

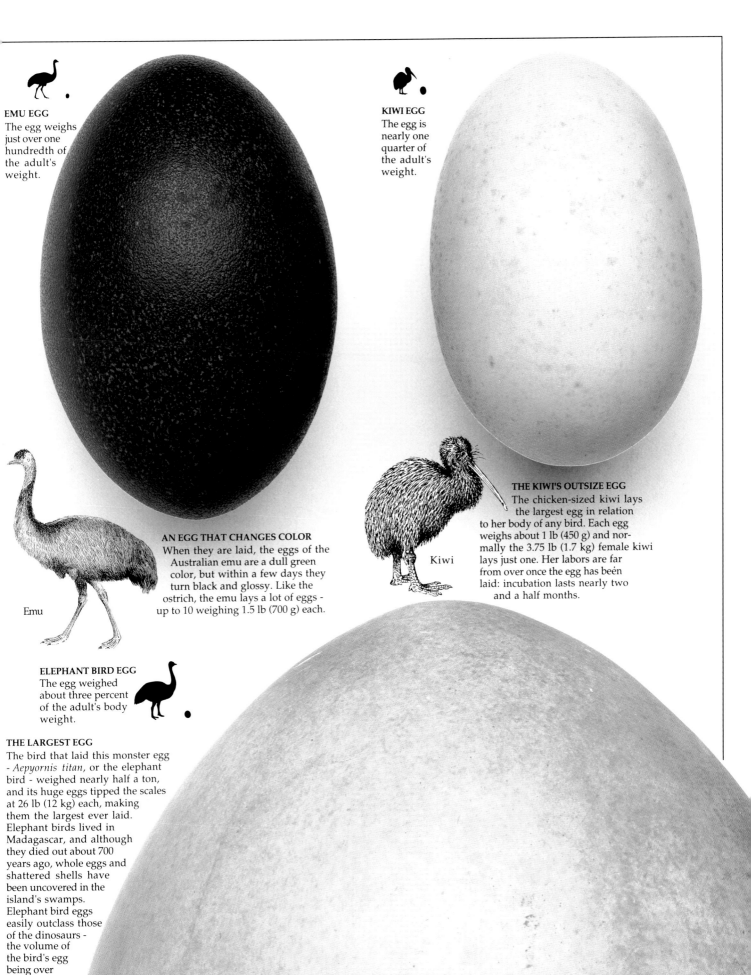

EMU EGG
The egg weighs just over one hundredth of the adult's weight.

KIWI EGG
The egg is nearly one quarter of the adult's weight.

AN EGG THAT CHANGES COLOR
When they are laid, the eggs of the Australian emu are a dull green color, but within a few days they turn black and glossy. Like the ostrich, the emu lays a lot of eggs - up to 10 weighing 1.5 lb (700 g) each.

Emu

THE KIWI'S OUTSIZE EGG
The chicken-sized kiwi lays the largest egg in relation to her body of any bird. Each egg weighs about 1 lb (450 g) and normally the 3.75 lb (1.7 kg) female kiwi lays just one. Her labors are far from over once the egg has been laid: incubation lasts nearly two and a half months.

Kiwi

ELEPHANT BIRD EGG
The egg weighed about three percent of the adult's body weight.

THE LARGEST EGG
The bird that laid this monster egg - *Aepyornis titan*, or the elephant bird - weighed nearly half a ton, and its huge eggs tipped the scales at 26 lb (12 kg) each, making them the largest ever laid. Elephant birds lived in Madagascar, and although they died out about 700 years ago, whole eggs and shattered shells have been uncovered in the island's swamps. Elephant bird eggs easily outclass those of the dinosaurs - the volume of the bird's egg being over twice that of any dinosaur egg.

Hatching

FOR SOMETHING SO LIGHT, the shell of an egg is extremely strong, and a hatching bird must spend hours or even days of hard labor in breaking this barrier to the outside world. Some birds hatch in a poorly developed state. As nestlings, they are helpless and depend completely on their parents for food. However, "precocial" birds, such as the pheasant shown here, are well developed on hatching and can soon fend for themselves.

INSIDE THE EGG
Development of the embryo starts as soon as the mother begins incubation.

Albumen
Yolk
1
Embryo
Protein cord

Air sac
2
Sac for waste products
Embryo

Developing chick
3
Shrinking yolk sac

1 PREPARING FOR HATCHING
Hatching for a pheasant chick, like that of other birds, begins invisibly. The chick, still completely enclosed in the shell, turns around so that its beak is pointing toward the egg's blunt end. Then, with a sudden movement of its head, it pecks at the air sac. This is a crucial part of the chick's development because, by breaking into the sac, the chick is able to breathe air for the first time. Once its lungs are functioning, the chick may call to its mother from inside the egg. These calls probably help to prepare her for the onset of hatching.

4 COMPLETING THE CIRCLE
By hammering away at the shell, the chick has now almost detached the blunt end from the rest of the egg. Large pieces of shell fall away from the egg as the chick struggles to finish its labors. An entire clutch of pheasant eggs hatches within a few hours, so by the time the chick has reached this stage, many of its brothers and sisters may have already hatched.

5 GETTING A GRIP
Having cut a complete circle through the shell, the chick begins to emerge from the egg. From now on, things happen very quickly. The chick first hooks its toes over the lip of the shell (the toes are just visible here), and then, having gotten a good grip, it starts to push with its feet and shoulders. With a few heaves, the egg's blunt end is lifted away.

2 BREAKING THE SHELL

Hatching begins in earnest when, after several attempts, the chick finally breaks through the shell. It does this with the help of two special adaptations. The first is the "egg tooth," a small projection on its beak that breaks the shell and falls off soon after hatching. The second is a powerful muscle behind the head that powers the egg tooth's blows. Between pecking sessions, the chick stops for long rests.

3 CUTTING A CIRCLE

Having broken open the shell, the chick sets about extending the initial crack sideways. After each bout of pecking, it stops and turns itself slightly by pushing with its feet. The chick's repeated pecking and turning produces a crack that runs neatly around the base of the egg's blunt end. This will eventually allow the blunt end to be pushed away.

— Egg tooth

6 BREAKING OUT

With its feet clearly visible, the chick gives another push and the blunt end of the egg comes away, sitting like a hat on the chick's head. This method of hatching, with the head emerging first, is shared by nearly all birds. The only exceptions are a few waders and other ground-living birds, which either smash open their eggs in random pieces or kick their way out feet first.

7 INTO THE OUTSIDE WORLD

With a final push, the chick tumbles out of the shell that has protected it during the three and a half weeks of incubation. Within the next two hours, its feathers will dry and fluff up to provide an insulating jacket that will keep it warm. Once that has happened, the race is on to feed and grow. Pheasant chicks leave their nest almost immediately, and, amazing though it may seem, they are able to fly in only two weeks.

Growing up

Ground-nesting birds hatch in a well-developed state (p. 56). However, the newly hatched young of many tree- and hole-nesting birds are little more than baglike feeding machines. They have well-developed digestive systems, but everything else about them - including their eyes - is unfinished. This does not last for long. Fueled by a staggering supply of food, nestlings like the blue tit's grow at a great rate. The young of many species increase their weight by ten times in as many days, and their development is so rapid that they quickly catch up with birds that hatch with all their feathers.

Wing

Leg

Joined eyelids

Mouth brightly colored to attract attention

Feather tufts

Feather tract *Feather sheaths*

1 ONE DAY OLD
Twenty-four hours after hatching, blue tit nestlings have no feathers and their eyes are closed. During the day, both parents leave the nestlings to search for food. However, the young never remain on their own for long, because their parents return to the nest with food every few minutes. The parents may make up to 1,000 trips between them per day.

BIRD OF GOOD OMEN
Faithful to its mate and tireless as a parent, the stork is recognized internationally as a symbol of the birth of a new human baby.

2 THREE DAYS OLD
In a scene all too familiar to their weary parents, the growing nestlings beg for food. Their instinctive reaction is set off by their parents' arrival at the nest, or sometimes by the parents' calls. By the third day, small tufts of feathers have appeared, and the nestlings are about four times heavier than when they hatched.

3 FIVE DAYS OLD
By this time, dark gray feather tracts have appeared down the nestlings' backs and on their wings. These are the areas of skin that will produce feathers. On the wings, the tubelike sheaths that will eventually produce and protect the flight feathers have already started to develop.

Feather sheaths

Emerging feather tips

ESCAPE FROM DANGER
Although most birds protect their nestlings by bluff or aggression when threatened, some parents can pick up their young and carry them away. Depending on the species, they may use either their beak, legs, or talons.

EMERGENCY AIRLIFT
The woodcock is said to hold a chick between its legs while flying, although this has never been proved.

PINCER MOVEMENT
The secretive water rail carries its chicks in its long beak.

CARRIED IN TALONS
Some birds of prey, like the hawk, are thought to hold their nestlings in their talons.

4 NINE DAYS OLD
As the feather sheaths grow longer, the tips of the flight feathers themselves start to emerge. The areas of bare skin between the feather tracts have started to disappear, covered up by the growing feathers. The nest is starting to get crowded, although by blue tit standards, five nestlings is a relatively small family.

5 THIRTEEN DAYS OLD
At nearly two weeks, the nestlings are fully feathered and their eyes are open. Within another five days they will leave the nest, but the young birds will follow their parents for some time, begging for food as they gradually learn how to look after themselves. Full independence often comes when the parents begin preparations for another clutch of eggs. Once the young birds find that their parents are ignoring their calls for food, they fend for themselves.

Attracting birds

IN WINTER, A ROOSTING BIRD like a robin can burn up a tenth of its body weight just in order to stay alive during the long hours of darkness. With each chilly daybreak, the hungry bird must find food soon or die, so there is no better way to attract birds into your backyard than by providing a regular supply of winter food. Seeds, nuts, fat, kitchen scraps, and water will not only help the birds but will also enable you to watch them at close quarters. Having kept your backyard birds alive during the winter, you can persuade many to stay for the summer by giving them somewhere to nest. As wild habitats disappear, nest boxes placed carefully beyond the reach of cats make valuable homes for a variety of birds.

Great and blue tits are attracted by nuts and fat at bird tables

CALL OF THE WILD
Birds have an instinctive distrust of humans, but St. Francis of Assisi (here portrayed in stained glass) is said to have had a special attraction for birds.

Sloping lid to throw off rainwater

Hole 1.14 in (29 mm) across keeps out large birds

Perching post

Hinged lid for inspecting nest

OPEN-FRONT BOXES
Robins, flycatchers, wrens, and wagtails prefer nest boxes that give them a good view when incubating. These birds usually nest in thick vegetation, so the box needs to be well concealed. This will also help to protect the birds from cats.

GABLED BOXES
A roof gives nestlings protection aginst rain, but it also reduces air circulation. Nest boxes should not be placed where they will be in direct sunlight.

SIMPLE HOLE-FRONTED BOXES
This straightforward design appeals to woodland birds such as tits and nuthatches. The small hole keeps out inquisitive sparrows.

FANCY BOXES
What appeals to humans doesn't necessarily appeal to birds. Bird boxes with unnecessary decorations may put birds off looking for a home. If you do choose a "house box" like this first make sure that it is solidly built. Then check that it can be cleaned and that the roof really will keep rainwater out of the nesting chamber.

Removable lid for inspecting nest

Two halves of a log hollowed out and nailed together to make the nesting chamber

LOG BOXES
A hollowed-out log makes an excellent home for small woodland birds. This box does not have a perching post, but the bark around the entrance hole is rough enough to give a bird a good toe-hold when landing or taking off.

Feeding table may attract other birds, disturbing those nesting in the box

SEED CAKES AND PUDDINGS

Of all the kinds of food that you can give backyard birds, oils and fats are the best sources of energy. All seeds have oils in them, but they can be pressed together with more oil or fat to make a real bird banquet. This way of feeding birds has another advantage. Because the food is in a solid lump, birds cannot fly away with it, giving you plenty of opportunity to watch them at their meal.

Fat and seed ball

MEALWORMS

Insect-eating birds find these beetle grubs quite irresistible. Mealworms can be raised in containers filled with bran.

Great spotted woodpecker feeding on peanuts

Screw-fit lid for refilling

Peanuts

Wire mesh keeping nuts in and large birds out

Perching post

Commercial "bird pudding"

Seed cake

Coconut, a winter food for acrobatic blue tits

LOOSE SEED

Mixtures of loose seed are an excellent food, although birds such as tits may fly away with the larger seeds and eat them out of sight.

Hunger sometimes forces birds to overcome shyness in winter

NUT DISPENSER

Natural, *unsalted* peanuts are popular with tits and greenfinches. A hanging dispenser helps to keep larger birds at bay.

BREAD

Although not an ideal food for birds, bread makes a useful stopgap. Brown bread makes a far better bird food than white.

Watching birds

I<small>N NORTH AMERICA ALONE</small>, including annual migrants, there are about 900 species of birds. An experienced bird watcher may recognize any one of these given no more than a distant silhouette or just a few seconds of song. This skill can seem baffling, but it is simply the result of careful observation - looking at the shape and color of birds and also watching the way they live.

Getting close to wild birds requires skill and patience

WARNING
When watching birds, always avoid disturbing them. Be especially careful when watching or photographing parent birds with their young.

KEEPING A NOTEBOOK
Field guides are essential for identifying birds, but keeping a notebook is the best way to train your eye to look for a bird's key features. Sketching plumage and flight patterns and noting behavior will all help to build up your knowledge.

SKETCHING EQUIPMENT
You don't have to be an artist to draw birds. A collection of colored pencils will enable you to sketch details instead of writing lengthy notes

Objective lens

Ruler for measuring feathers

Eyepiece lens

BINOCULARS
Serious bird watching is almost impossible without a good pair of binoculars, but good does not necessarily mean tremendously powerful. For bird watching, binoculars should be light and have good magnification together with a fairly wide field of view. Heavy binoculars are hard to carry and use, and if they magnify more than 10 times, the field of view is narrow and the image very wobbly - this can make locating moving birds very difficult. Binoculars are graded by the diameter of the objective lens and the magnification. One of the best combinations of size and magnification for bird watching is the 8 x 30

Magnifying glass

Plastic tweezers are less likely to damage fine bones than metal ones

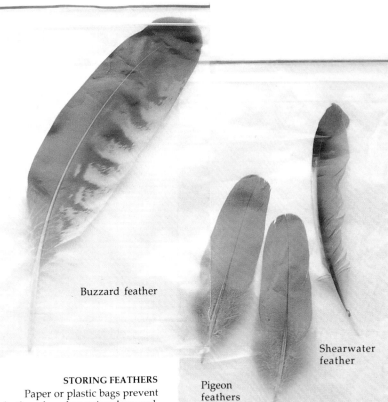

STORING FEATHERS
Paper or plastic bags prevent feathers from becoming damaged.

Buzzard feather

Pigeon feathers

Shearwater feather

EQUIPMENT FOR EXAMINING PELLETS
Many of the animal remains inside bird pellets (p. 42) are very delicate and are easily damaged when a pellet is pulled apart. By using a magnifying glass and a pair of tweezers, small bones and teeth can be separated from fur and feathers without breakage.

Camera mounting

TRIPOD
Cameras that use high-power lenses need a steady support to keep the image from wobbling. A lightweight tripod is essential. It can also be used with binoculars.

USING A "HIDE"
Birds are quick to detect movement but will ignore nonmoving objects, no matter how out of place they seem to human eyes. Even on flat, open ground birds will accept a "hide" as a natural feature and approach it without any fear.

CHOOSING LENSES
With a standard 50 mm lens, birds often appear small and indistinct. A telephoto lens produces a much larger image.

CAMERAS FOR BIRD PHOTOGRAPHY
A 35 mm SLR (single-lens reflex) camera is ideal for photographing birds because the image can be seen exactly through the viewfinder. Taking pictures of wild birds - especially in flight - *is* difficult. Practice approaching the subject, focusing quickly, and steadying the camera - before going farther afield.

200 mm tele-photo lens

Index

Acknowledgments

Dorling Kindersley would like to thank:
Philip Amies; the staff of the Natural History Department, City of Bristol Museum; the staff of the British Museum (Natural History) at Tring; Martin Brown of the Wildfowl Trust, Slimbridge; and Rosemary Crawford for their advice and invaluable help in providing specimens.
Steve Parker and Anne-Marie Bulat for their work on the initial stages of the book.
Fred Ford and Mike Pilley of Radius Graphics, and Ray Owen and Nick Madren for artwork.
Tim Hammond for editorial assistance.

Publishers' note
No bird has been injured or in any way harmed during the preparation of this book.

Picture credits
t=top b= bottom m= middle l=left r=right

R. Austing/Frank Lane Picture Agency: 32br
A.P. Barnes/Planet Earth Pictures: 15m
Jen & Des Bartlett/ Survival Anglia: 54br
Leo Batten/Frank Lane Picture Agency: 39m
G.I. Bernard/NHPA: 21ml, mr
Tony & Liz Bomford/Ardea London: 14mr
Bridgeman Art Library: 13tr; 28tr; 52t; 61b
C. Carvalho/Frank Lane Picture Agency: 17t
Manfred Danegger/NHPA: 13m
Mary Evans Picture Library: 6bl, br; 9 tr, mr; 10t, mr, b; 20bl; 24t; 26t; 30mr; 32m; 36t, mr; 38t; 41t; 54tl, tr, bl; 56t; 58b
J. K. Fawcett/Frank Lane Picture Agency: 12mr
Jeff Foott/Survival Anglia: 31mr

T. & P. Gardner/Frank Lane Picture Agency: 21bl
Sonia Halliday: 60tr
Brian Hawkes/Robert Harding: 47t
John Hawkins/Eric & David Hosking: 13tl; 19tl; 35m
Peggy Heard/Frank Lane Picture Agency: 61m
David Hosking: 16t; 35tr; 37bl; 47m; 60m
Eric Hosking: 33b; 63
Eric & David Hosking: 12bl; 14m; 29t, ml; 37tl; 46m
Roger Hosking/Eric & David Hosking: 60tl
Hellio & Van Ingen/NHPA: 40b
R. Jones/Frank Lane Picture Agency: 17m
Frank W. Lane: 37mr
Gordon Langsbury/Bruce Coleman Ltd: 13b; 14b
Michael Leach/NHPA: 34m
Mansell Collection; 6t, 10ml; 34t; 54m
Pickthall Library: 15t
Press-Tige Pictures: 12mr
Derek A. Robinson/Frank Lane Picture Agency: 8m; 47b

H. Schrempp/Frank Lane Picture Agency: 32bl
Sinclair Stammers/Science Photo Library: 6m
Roger Tidman/Frank Lane Picture Agency: 37tr
B.S. Turner/ Frank Lane Picture Agency: 42t
R. Van Nostrand/Frank Lane Picture Agency: 37br
John Watkins/Frank Lane Picture Agency: 33ml
Philip Wayre/NHPA: 19br
Roger Wilmshurt/Bruce Coleman Ltd: 15b
Roger Wilmshurst/Frank Lane Picture Agency; 12br; 46t; 49t
W. Wisniewski/Frank Lane Picture Agency: 37ml
J. Zimmermann/Frank Lane Picture Agency: 31tr; 36b

Illustrations by: Mick Loates of Linden Artists, Coral Mula and Will Giles.

Picture research by: Millie Trowbridge.